J. S. WADE
15 PORTLAND ST.
LITTLE ROCK, ARK. 72212

SCHOOLS OF THE FUTURE

SCHOOLS OF THE FUTURE:

How American Business and Education Can Cooperate to Save Our Schools

MARVIN J. CETRON

WITH *BARBARA SORIANO*
AND *MARGARET GAYLE*

Sponsored by:
American Association of School Administrators

McGRAW-HILL BOOK COMPANY
New York   St. Louis   San Francisco
Toronto   Hamburg   Mexico

This book is dedicated to the dedicated teachers of Lebanon, Pennsylvania, Brooklyn, New York, and Fairfax County, Virginia—teachers to my family.

Marvin J. Cetron

To Adan and Adriana and the schools of their future.

Barbara R. S. Soriano

To my greatest teachers—my parents, husband, and four daughters who taught me how to live, love, and to value the future for all people.

Margaret E. Gayle

1 2 3 4 5 6 7 8 9 D O C D O C 8 7 6 5

ISBN 0-07-010350-X

Library of Congress Cataloging in Publication Data

Cetron, Marvin J.
    Schools of the future.
    1. Education—United States—Forecasting.
    2. Continuing education—United States—Forecasting.
    3. Vocational education—United States—Forecasting.
    4. Occupational retraining—United States—Forecasting.
    I. Soriano, Barbara. II. Gayle, Margaret. III. American
    Association of School Administrators. IV. Title.
    LA217.C4   1985   370'.973   84-28871
    ISBN 0-07-010350-X

Book design by Mary A. Wirth

FOUNDATION FUND
AMERICAN ASSOCIATION OF SCHOOL ADMINISTRATORS

This study of the future of education was conducted for the American Association of School Administrators by Forecasting International, Marvin J. Cetron, President. The views expressed do not necessarily reflect the positions or opinions of the American Association of School Administrators, its members, staff, Executive Committee or Foundation Fund Board of Trustees. This study does, however, provide insights into a number of issues and possible events that should be considered by all schools as they plan for the future.

We wish to express our appreciation to the Foundation Fund trustees for their advice and encouragement:

Anne Dees served as editorial liaison for the AASA Communications Department; Gary Marx served as project director.

CONTENTS

INTRODUCTION / 1
1. / Today's Schools: Common Myths—Future Reality / 5
2. / The New School: A Future Scenario / 14
3. / Technology in Future Society and Future Schools / 25
SCENARIOS:
4. / Future Lifestyles / 37
Demographic Charts / 44
5. / 21st-Century Women, Families, and the Schools / 66
6. / Minorities and Schools of the Future / 73
7. / Funding / 78
8. / School/Business Partnerships of Today and
Tomorrow / 85
9. / Longer School Day and Year / 92
10. / Low Pupil-Teacher Ratios / 99
11. / Curriculum and Student Standards / 102
12. / Teaching and Professional Standards / 110
Epilogue / 121
APPENDIX A: Future Conditions—Implications
for School Planners / 123
APPENDIX B: The National Education Reform
Reports / 145
Acknowledgments / 159
Index / 161

INTRODUCTION

The students who will graduate from high school in the year 2000 will be entering elementary school in less than 3 years. The schools that will guide these students—and shape our nation's future in the 21st century—are being planned today, at a time when education is again in the national spotlight. Nearly 30 reports issued by commissions, task forces, and individuals have made it clear to the American people that their nation will be "at risk" unless they pay attention to their schools.

During the past several years, dozens of panels, commissions, and other experts have made recommendations on how schools can become more effective. A chart showing an overview of all these recommendations is included in Appendix B.

Some of the recommendations will work in some communities and not in others. Some are based on sound research and some are not, but all grow out of the same basic belief: that continuing to improve America's schools is the key to the United States's future. So during this time of reassessment and reevaluation, schools have an opportunity—and a responsibility—to improve and gain needed support. To make the most of the attention currently focused on education, schools must rally their communities and staffs to formulate plans.

That is why the American Association of School Administrators commissioned Forecasting International to conduct this study. Schools must make their plans for the future with an understanding of the key issues that will affect education in their communities. A number of these are identified and discussed in this book. School leaders across the nation were asked to judge the probability and potential impact of a number of possible events. Those events and trends judged to be significant in shaping America's schools in the next 20 years are the ones on which this book will concentrate.

- A major responsibility of schools in the future will be to prepare students to enter a rapidly changing job market. If the United States is to continue to compete in the worldwide marketplace, American workers will need to be more highly trained than at present.
- Schools will be responsible for preparing students who are adaptable, who are able to respond quickly to the changing requirements of new technologies. In the near future, workers' jobs will change dramatically every 5 to 10 years. Schools will train both youth and adults; adult workers will need reeducation and retraining whenever business and industry update their operations. In the future, workers will be displaced frequently and they will be moving constantly from one occupation to another. They will need periodic retraining because each new job will be different from the previous one.
- By the year 1990 or 2000, public schools should be training both young and adult students for work. But before they can do this, two major changes will have to be made. First, funds must be available to enable schools to operate these job-training programs and to help them adapt physically to these new demands. Second, educational planners must ensure that schools will be open when adults can attend them. These two changes will mean that the entire school day and school plant will be restructured—not piece by piece, but altogether.
- In the future, schools and businesses will need to work closely in a new business/education partnership. In many cases, the private sector will supply the funds that schools need to expand their programs. Sometimes businesses will actually purchase services—such as training programs for workers—from the schools.

Business leaders will also advise the schools about the changing needs of the marketplace to ensure that the students who enter the work force have the best preparation possible.

- Emphasis on such "traditional" academic subjects as reading, writing, and mathematics will increase—not decrease. Students will need these skills to help them adapt to being retrained every 5 to 10 years. They will also need to communicate more effectively than ever before.
- New technologies, such as computers, videodiscs, and cable television will change the look of the "schoolroom." In the future, students may spend 1 or 2 days each week studying at home. Increased and well-planned use of these new learning technologies will enable machines and humans each to teach what they teach best.
- Because of the additional responsibilities that will be imposed on teachers, they will achieve greater status in American society. In the future, teachers will be paid salaries that are comparable with other professionals. They will work in schools that offer continuing opportunities for professional advancement and training. As a result, education will once again attract the nation's brightest and most qualified students.

The planning to make these predictions a reality must begin now. And everyone in the community must take the responsibility for change. Citizens need to become informed and involved with the decisions that affect their local schools.

This book contains information, ideas, and forecasts that can help schools and citizens come together to plan for the future. The first three chapters set forth a general picture of the trends that will shape schools in the future. Ten key trends are then discussed in greater detail, depicting how education might evolve in 1990 and in 2000.

Before anything can be planned or accomplished, however, realities about education must be separated from myths. Chapter One identifies many common misconceptions and points up present circumstances that will impinge on future educational developments.

We have forecast a basically positive, progressive future for America's schools based on current international and national economic and social trends. These trends could change direction, however, thereby altering our predictions. But nothing will alter these forecasts as greatly as inaction. If America's citizens ignore these warnings about their educational and industrial future, the United States's economic stability and preeminence will be jeopardized.

1

TODAY'S SCHOOLS: COMMON
MYTHS—FUTURE REALITY

As the U.S. government and many communities now look to change
schools in dramatic ways, the criteria for these decisions to revise
and restructure the system should be examined. Are current assumptions about both the positive and negative aspects of the nation's
schools valid or are they myths? Some controversial issues relevant
to the reform movement in the public schools are discussed below.

MYTH Reforms recommended in *A Nation at Risk* and nearly 30
other critiques have been put into effect on a nationwide basis.

REALITY Efforts to improve the schools are just beginning in many
parts of the nation. In *A Nation Responds*, a follow-up to *A Nation
at Risk*, the U.S. Department of Education notes that 32 states have
taken important action.

But *A Nation Responds* sometimes confuses talk with well-planned
action. For example, if one school district in a state instituted a
training program in robotics, the report credited the whole state with
this improvement. If business and school leaders met three times,
some follow-up stories implied that suddenly a new coalition of business and education had been forged.

Since 1983, over 30 states have raised academic standards, and
more states have such legislation pending. Raising academic standards
is not effective, however, unless programs are initiated to help students achieve these new standards. In the same light, strengthening

/ 5

teacher accountability standards will work only if evaluation procedures are improved. At present, funding for such supportive programs has been scanty and cannot sustain a continuous effort.

If public education is not changed to make it useful and valuable to its students, an even greater crisis than the present one will occur. There will be massive dropouts, causing a shortage of both vocationally trained and college-eligible students. As a result, the employable pool of educated workers will decrease and America's technological edge will be blunted. If reform is not aggressively pursued in the schools, U.S. productivity will diminish even more than it has and the nation will be worse off than before.

Nevertheless, some schools and communities will be able to effect change more quickly and thoroughly than others. Those that have begun are already ahead of the game.

MYTH   The education reform reports take into account students of all levels of academic ability.

REALITY   Reports have dealt primarily with the 25%–30% of high school students headed for college. They have devoted far less attention to other students, particularly adults who will need job training in the future if they are to remain in the labor force.

Approximately three-fourths of future jobs may not require a traditional college education. Instead, many high-technology jobs will require specific technical training lasting 1 or 2 years. Many high schools may provide this training either in school or on the job site. Adults will comprise the greatest number of this new student body. As we mentioned previously, in order for the United States to maintain its leadership in the future, industry and business will need to update their technological equipment and procedures every 5 to 10 years. Retraining the adult work force will be essential. Some workers will simply learn to handle new systems or equipment. Others will have to master new vocations as old ones disappear.

The students of tomorrow will still attend twelve or more years of school during their youth, but every 5 to 10 years after that they will need additional schooling and retraining. Public schools will become a major base for this retraining.

MYTH   Even though basic literacy is a problem for U.S. youth, most adults have the ability to read and write a simple sentence.

REALITY The real question is not whether adults are literate; it is how literate they are. In 1977, the University of Texas did a national survey to determine what sort of skills were needed to function in everyday life—reading a job application; filling out government forms; shopping for clothes, groceries, and medicine; and working in entry-level, unskilled jobs. Using their definitions of literacy, the University of Texas found that 60% of America's adult population cannot read and compute well enough to go through their everyday lives without difficulty.

These adults might find it difficult to train or retrain for available jobs. Schools must provide leadership in dealing with this lack of basic literacy. The gap between what these adults can do and what they should be able to do will only widen as the literacy requirements of high-technology society increase and as literacy itself is redefined.

MYTH Students belong in the schoolroom, where they should be taught concepts rather than specific applications, especially at a time when the job market is changing so rapidly. They should learn about jobs *after* they leave high school, when they enter the working world.

REALITY When students wait to work until after graduation, they are hurting themselves economically. They certainly are missing an opportunity to gain job experience and establish themselves in the job market. Twenty-five percent of the nation's high school graduates were unemployed in 1984. This shocking statistic is due in part, we feel, to the students' lack of knowledge of specific job skills. Of course, students must learn concepts and schools will continue to teach them a traditionally broad liberal arts curriculum. But at about the eighth grade, many students can benefit from school-guided part-time work and, in the future, schools will provide this. Many students will discover, for instance, that they can use trigonometry on the job; they will have the opportunity to write simple newspaper articles or advertising copy for a telemarketing business. They might also use basic arithmetic as bookkeepers' assistants or observe biological and chemical principles as hospital aides. As businesses join schools in preparing students, the academic curriculum will broaden and change.

Students learn to reason more effectively when in practical rather than academic settings, when they are shown how general concepts apply to specific problems. What better way to master an idea than to use it in a real-world situation where students can see a purpose for learning it? The actual application of ideas to concrete situations will sharpen their desire to learn and guide them toward suitable careers.

Both on the job and at school the emphasis will be on how to think: how to use information and how to work in teams to solve problems. These teams will be much like those in many manufacturing areas today. Students, in turn, may gather information, enter it into the computer, and work with others to evaluate it.

Dependability and teamwork at school will pay off on the job. A Johns Hopkins University study shows that employers are interested in dependability and in how well students accept supervision, work together, and show initiative. Students will have the opportunity to learn other skills as they periodically return to school for retraining and to prepare to move up the career ladder.

MYTH Teaching job training in the schools is a waste of time since jobs in the future will be changing so frequently because of technological advances.

REALITY The skills needed for jobs today are changing and will continue to change in the future. For example, the half-life of the skills an engineer learns in college today is 5 years; new knowledge will replace much of what he or she knows.

But job obsolescence is not a major factor if the population has been well educated to start with. Although the first high-tech job may require 1 or 2 years of training, the next job often less than a year to learn.

MYTH Computer skills and related technological skills will make students successful in the job market of the future. It will be unnecessary to provide a general academic education since it will have no bearing upon what students will be doing in their prospective jobs.

REALITY Future workers, even in the technical jobs that will make up more than three-fourths of the job market, will need to have the traditional skills that public education once provided. As jobs change in the future, it will become necessary for a worker to read increasingly complex materials, write more persuasively than in the past, and use basic principles of math and science with ease. Traditional, basic literacy skills will only increase in importance.

MYTH The most intelligent students in a class should be singled out to receive special attention, since it is they who ultimately will develop new products, technological advances, and industries.

REALITY Creativity is only moderately related to intelligence. Up to about 120 IQ, there seems to be a strong correlation. After that, students with high IQs often become quite narrowly focused and sometimes lose the flexibility necessary for creative problem-solving.

Over the next 15 years, tremendous gains should be made in understanding how the brain develops and why students excel in one area of endeavor, but not in others. Students will be categorized not by IQ, but by different learning behaviors and abilities. They will move from one problem-solving group to another based on their potential for development of various job skills, their creative skills, and their group interaction skills—not solely because of academic strength.

MYTH The best way to teach a student whose first language is other than English is to teach him/her in his own language first and in English second. It is a double burden for a student to learn new concepts at the same time he or she is learning a new language.

REALITY For most students, training in English first may work best. The decision rests on several factors: the age of the student, what the first language is used for versus what English will be used for, what role the home language has in the student's surrounding community, and how the decision will affect his or her self-esteem. Self-esteem may be one of the most important considerations. Some Hmong students from the hills of Cambodia, who come to this country with little experience in schooling, may find the formal classroom situation strange and intimidating. Very young Hispanic students may adapt easily to a new language. Adult foreign language speakers on the other hand come to school to learn English; they do not need help in maintaining their home language. By the year 2000, through the use of videodiscs and simulation for language instruction, students will find themselves beginning to use English more quickly than they can now.

MYTH Employers make no distinction between white and black high school graduates when hiring. They are more concerned about whether the students have graduated from a good high school.

REALITY According to a Johns Hopkins University study, employers prefer to hire blacks who attended suburban high schools over blacks who attended inner-city schools of all-minority populations. Apparently these employers feel that suburban students will be "better long-term risks," having come from racially integrated schools with populations comparable to those found in most business settings. Hence, the location of his or her high school directly affects a black student's chances for employment.

MYTH Computer education in public schools will enable poor school districts to offer educational programs equal in excellence to rich school districts.

REALITY Computers in the schools will not affect academic achievement as much as computers in the home. Even though 53% of our nation's schools now have computers, there still aren't enough for children to learn effectively on them. By 1995, most households will own a computer for educational purposes, but only by the year 2005 or 2010 will computers be as commonly distributed and accessible in schools. Parents—not schools—will determine initially how computers will affect education.

Therefore, in these early stages there will be greater differences between rich and poor schools because of computer education. The children of parents who stress educational uses of computers will simply move faster academically than children whose parents lack the machinery.

Initial information from a 1984 study by Future Computing, Inc., however, shows that lower-income families have bought computers at a greater rate than upper-income families. If the prices of both computers and software become affordable to the general public, poorer families will buy educational packages—as they have bought encyclopedias, dictionaries, and educational toys—at great sacrifice and on installment plans. Schools will need to advise interested families on educational software and should even provide them with access to computers.

MYTH Education should remain, for the most part, the sole province of the teachers, since they are best equipped to decide what to teach and how to teach it.

REALITY Studies indicate that the most effective schools are those in which school administrators and teachers work as a team. Further, they actively involve the community in setting goals, implementing programs, and evaluating results. This means more than just the once-a-month PTA meeting. It means that community members—local business people as well as parents—are actually in the school every day: they help teach; they share with educators their perceptions about what seems wrong and right; teachers and administrators are responsive to them. This cooperation is even now being implemented as policy through contracts among businesses, local governments, and schools in cities such as St. Paul, Houston, and Boston. This trend is likely to continue.

Schools of the future will build upon these relationships. Curriculum committees will be composed of educators, parents, and possibly business representatives. Some technical or business classes may be taught by experts, whose progress and results will be monitored by educators. Classes may meet outside the school building to suit the needs of the businesses involved or to reinforce lessons learned.

MYTH Schools will continue to use volunteers to manage and operate athletic, tutorial, and extracurricular programs.

REALITY Nearly four-fifths (79%) of our public schools use volunteers as teachers and coaches; more than 4.3 million people volunteer part time, according to the National Center for Educational Statistics. But these programs are not easy to run nor are they free. Volunteers often require paid professional direction—training, supervision, encouragement, and recognition—in their unpaid positions. The key to good programs, as shown in a 1981 National Center for Educational Statistics survey, is hiring full-time volunteer coordinators, for school volunteer programs can be the most effective tool for gaining community support. The volunteers' involvement results in their feeling pride in as well as responsibility for their schools; volunteers become active in supporting funding increases from local government and business.

As more women enter the work force and as older adults become involved in their own educational efforts, however, schools will need to provide different incentives to expand their volunteer groups. At present, schools ask for parent volunteers. In the future, schools will have to seek volunteers from the community as a whole, whose members will respond if they can gain valuable job experience they otherwise might not be able to obtain. Senior citizens are becoming the largest single group of volunteers and will continue to be so in the near future.

MYTH   Merit-pay plans will improve the performance of teachers.

REALITY   Merit-pay plans could improve teacher performance if there were enough money to reward all those who put forth extra effort and get better results. When only a few good teachers may be rewarded, others may not make the extra effort. Better student performance evaluation techniques are needed to make a merit-pay program effective.

Merit-pay plans might also improve the performance of teachers if these plans were not used as substitutes for general pay increases. Teachers are the lowest-paid professional group whose jobs require at least a bachelor's degree. Merit pay is not a substitute for salary parity. Industry demand in particular will be a major market force behind the increase in teachers' salaries. Businesses have already begun to purchase teacher services from schools and they will continue to compete with schools to hire teachers with high-tech skills.

MYTH   Divorced or single working mothers are not as supportive of the schools as stay-at-home married mothers.

REALITY   A recent study by Johns Hopkins has shown that divorced and single working mothers spend more minutes helping their children at home than married stay-at-home mothers. On the other hand, nonworking mothers volunteer more time at school than working mothers. Because schools see stay-at-home mothers more often, they have assumed that working mothers are not as supportive.

As more women enter the work force and the number of single, working parents increases, schools cannot continue to judge parents' support solely on the basis of traditional assumptions. Schools must develop a rapport not only with parents who appear at the school door, but with those whose schedules make visits difficult.

MYTH   Computers will actually bring families closer together. When parents work at home and students study at home 1 or 2 days a week using the computer links to the school, family harmony will increase.

REALITY   In studies of marriages where both spouses worked at home it was found that the divorce rate quadrupled. The resulting friction between husband and wife, parents and children, all trying to work in the same place, perhaps with the same equipment, could fracture the family peace. Schools will have to provide balanced schedules incorporating time at home, in the school building, and in the community. Community time could include neighborhood study groups, business internships, community service in volunteer citizen groups, and practice with the latest equipment in regional centers.

MYTH Schools can do little about dropouts. Such factors as broken homes, poverty, teenage pregnancy, and poor school grades cannot be avoided, even with intensive remedial classes. Once students have dropped out, it is even harder to get them back in school.

REALITY Schools can take major steps to prevent dropouts, even in poor neighborhoods and among pregnant teenage girls. Remedial academic programs do work in junior high school, particularly if materials for improving reading are suitable to each age group. Later on, work placement appears to be an important preventive measure.

Since there is a high probability that we will have an even greater dropout rate in the immediate future as school standards rise, schools must address the problem now. Programs must be offered to help students meet academic standards. Additionally, school-related job programs will be needed to stimulate student interest and success.

Work co-op programs that place students in part-time jobs and then forget about them are of marginal benefit. Schools must value the work and they must relate the academic day to the work day. Schools *can* tell which students are likely to drop out: They can watch grades. If in the first 6 weeks of an academic year a student's grades continue a pattern of decline from the year before, counseling should begin immediately.

If parents, business persons, public schools, and colleges recognize that they must work actively together, schools will be able to make needed changes. Participating in a planning group is a good place to start. Everyone must become involved in the change process, from beginning to end.

2

THE NEW SCHOOL: A FUTURE SCENARIO

MAJOR ITEMS AFFECTING FUTURE SCHOOLS

A number of factors will affect schools in the 21st century:
- Public schools will retrain workers making career changes, perhaps 3 or 4 times durings their working lives, due to high-tech.
- Minority populations will become the majority in most grade schools in the nation's large and middle-sized school districts.
- Computers will be available to students in prosperous districts on a 1:4 ratio.
- Federal grants will provide a major portion of the funding for job training and equipment (including computers) in poor school districts.
- Total employment will rise by 17% to 25% as the workweek declines to 32 hours (1990) and then 20–25 hours (2000).
- Women, particularly married women, will enter the work force at a faster rate than any other group within the population.
- More businesses will be involved in apprenticeship training.
- Older citizens (over 55) increasingly will participate in public school programs.
- A core, 9-month program will be offered in elementary and high schools, shifting electives to later in the lengthened day and to summer sessions.

• Teachers' salaries on an annual basis will be raised to within 10% of parity with other professionals requiring college degrees. The following scenario is a general one. Certain aspects of it may not occur in some local school districts, or may occur earlier or later than anticipated. Some school systems will be able to make changes more quickly than others. Some will be slow to bring adults into the school, slow to encourage women to enter business, slow to incorporate the computer as a major instructional tool.

Some schools in growing middle- or upper-middle-class suburban areas may be able to survive without enrolling adults. It will be unwise for them to do so, however. Adults choosing neighborhoods to move to and businesses looking for healthy growth environments and strong local teaching faculties to help them with job training will be making comparisons between progressive school districts and stultified ones. In the year 2000 adults will want strong schools for themselves and their parents, not only for their children.

The following scenario, then, is much more likely to occur in the year 2000 than in the year 1990. It is possible, however, if the general public becomes active in helping to make plans for their schools, that this entire scenario could occur before 1990.

As public schools respond to the challenge of integrating adults into the education system, they will restructure the entire school year. And it will be the public schools that respond: Universities and colleges will not be able to accommodate the great numbers of adults looking for retraining and an updated education. These higher education institutions will still concentrate on preparing students for developing future technological information, inventions, and industries.

THE SCENARIO

By 1990, most adults will be working a 32-hour week. During the time that they are not at work, many will be preparing for their next job. While the adult workweek is getting shorter, the student school week will be getting longer. Not only will the normal academic day be longer for children, but the buildings themselves will be open a minimum of 12 hours a day. Schools will be providing services to the community, to business, and to young students who will use the recreation facilities, computer lab, and job simulation stations—modules that combine computers, videodiscs, and instrumentation to duplicate job-work environments. Many schools may be open 24 hours a day. They will be training centers for adults from 4 P.M. to midnight; some will also serve business through their computer and communication facilities from midnight until the next morning when young students arrive again.

Individual communities may conduct classes that include both adults and high school students. But if for some reason this combination is unsuccessful, the groups can separate and work independently. In some communities adults might take over portions of school buildings that have been closed because of declining school enrollments.

At present, most schools are in session for approximately 180 days a year. A number of the reform reports recommend an increase to 210 days a year or 240 days to match schools abroad, but many people have objected. Monies have not been available; some students and teachers feel they do not have the mental energy for a longer year; and families want free time to make summer plans. Also, school buildings generally are not air-conditioned.

Schools in the 1990s, however, increasingly will extend the time buildings are in service. Air-conditioning and modifications in the size and purposes of classrooms will accommodate the changing purposes of school programs. Some students will have the option of accelerating their progress through the school year in order to graduate and enter college or the job market earlier. Others may spend time at school in the summer to enrich their academic backgrounds through telecommunications coursework with another school district, state, or country. Adults may find summer months a good time to train for a new phase of their careers. The core academic year will lengthen to 210 days, but students will not necessarily be in the school building at all times during this period.

STUDENTS WILL LEARN AT HOME OR IN THEIR COMMUNITIES, 1 OR 2 DAYS A WEEK

Interactive cable television and computer communication with the school may allow school districts to close down costly old buildings even if enrollments are increasing. As the workweek shortens from

32 hours a week in 1990 to 20–25 hours a week in the year 2000, families will want to make plans for the periods children would previously have been in school. Students will be able to time their study hours to fit these family schedules. The type of work they will be doing at home will be that best aided by the computer. The major difficulty preventing this move to home instruction in the 1980s is the inadequacy of present software. Eventually, computers will be used for the drill and practice of skills introduced by the teacher; they also will be used for helping students explore creative and problem-solving situations. Right now, however, software rarely does either job very well.

Teachers will effect some of the biggest changes in educational software. Their experience with computers in the classrooms during the late 1980s will give them insight into the ways software will need to change. The teachers who are particularly good at making modifications may even leave the classroom and launch their own software-writing businesses.

STUDENTS WILL HAVE INDIVIDUAL EDUCATION PLANS

Many teachers will operate in teaching teams. The team will be able to use frequently updated information on their students to design individual education plans (IEPs). In some school districts, these teams may be hired on a consulting rather than on a salaried basis. Schools will prescribe the standard of performance that is expected from the teaching team and if the standards are not met, their contracts will not be renewed.

IEPs are simply plans for instruction. Each student will have a plan tailored to his or her own background, interests, and skills. The IEPs in today's schools list skills in reading or math, for example, and suggest how the teacher should test the student to see if the skills have been mastered. IEPs in the future will also recommend whether students should learn each skill in a small or large group, independently, and/or with a teacher, one-on-one. They will suggest which senses the student should use more frequently to develop them further—for example, visual (reading books or computer screens) over aural (listening to tapes).

TEACHERS WILL TEACH DIFFERENTLY

After older students have acquired what are now described by educators as "minimum competencies" in various information areas—telling time, following directions, writing short essays, and the like, many will move from schools into the job world for part of the school week. (Lists of minimum competencies have been drawn up by state agencies in the 1970s and 1980s to define certain responsibilities of the school.)

Once the quality of computer software improves, schools will be able to teach and drill students in these minimum skills more efficiently, as well as increasing the percentage of students achieving certain minimum competencies. Some students will do so quickly, some more slowly. But much more flexibility with the teaching staff, with school resources, and with teaching strategies will be possible.

One of the major sources of flexibility will be in the ways teachers are assigned. Students who work relatively well on their own will be assigned to teachers who work well with large groups. Often lessons will be introduced and skills developed through teacher-managed computer systems. Teachers will be responsible for setting up the instructional schedules, reviewing progress with the students, and seeing that students have opportunities to participate in a broad range of learning situations: problem-solving groups; independent information-gathering activities in the school or the community; music, art, or drama activities led by professionals from these disciplines; or computer-based drill routines. For those who need to work in small groups, teachers skilled in handling and coordinating small-group experiences will move students from teacher-student interaction to student-student interaction. Students will teach each other, not because the teacher does not have time and is trying to find a way to keep these student teams busy, but because effective learning can take place in these teams.

In other words, teachers will be assigned students based on the kind of teaching they do best. Students will be assigned to groups based on the way they learn best. Some grouping will also be based on the subject to be taught. Students will not be assigned by grade level, but by the developmental level they have reached in each area. Neither teachers nor parents will be concerned with pupil-teacher ratios. It will not matter if students learn some subjects in groups of 30 and others alone. The amount of time students spend one-on-one with their teachers will be consistent with what learning researchers feel they need to be successful.

COMPUTER-BASED INSTRUCTION WILL SUPERSEDE CERTAIN TEXTBOOKS

As computer software improves, computers will begin to replace some kinds of textbooks; they already can replace drillbooks. Software can be tailored to meet individual student needs, and can be updated more quickly and inexpensively than textbooks. And computers can be linked with videodiscs or with equipment that simulates the job environment.

Computers themselves could even provide income for the school: Parents might come to school to learn how to use computers in their businesses, and companies could use school computer facilities to run their data at night.

Even without videodiscs and job-simulation equipment, computers will still be an important source of instruction. The writing and computing deficiencies that national education reform groups have noted may often be remedied by simple practice, something computers do tirelessly. When computer-assisted instruction was first heralded as the wave of the future in the early 1960s, the microcomputer was not available. Neither was friendly software, and the opportunity to modify software was limited. In the mid-1980s, we still lack the range of software necessary for computers to realize their promise, but the quality of software has improved during the last few years. As computer languages become more like people languages, teachers, among others, may more readily develop the needed software.

Computers linked with videodiscs will provide sight, sound, and movement. Some lessons in history, language, politics, psychology, math, word problems, and music, art, or dance could be taught or reinforced from one videodisc. Computer software, written by a member of a teaching team, will program sequences of visual images from a disc. The same computer program stops and starts the disc every so often to ask the student questions or to ask her or him to perform a function.

While widespread use of computer-linked equipment will not be a major feature of schools until the 21st century, certain schools will use computers in this way before 1995. Computer simulations of certain job procedures have been used to train employees for 10 years in certain industries. Because sophisticated workplace simulation equipment is expensive, it will probably be placed only in regional centers where students will be sent for short periods of time to study and live in supervised dormitories attached to the public school system. Finally, individual high schools will begin to offer simulation as a means of job training.

TEACHER PAY AND PERFORMANCE WILL BE RAISED

Before the mid-1990s, we predict that teachers will receive higher pay—to at least 90% of comparable professionals' salaries—and then will increase their pay as they measure up to increasingly stricter performance standards, or leave the field.

TEACHERS WILL WORK IN BUSINESS; BUSINESS WILL WORK IN SCHOOLS

Funding required to raise teachers' salaries will come in large part from businesses contracting to retrain their workers; from private individuals studying skills for their next jobs; from selling computer time, day-care, and geriatric services to the community; and from other ways of using school buildings more efficiently.

As business becomes more closely connected with schools, it is possible that skilled teachers will join private business in even greater numbers than they do today. Teachers may choose to continue their careers as trainers of employees for private businesses. Many times, however, businesses will find that teachers are valuable employees in other respects. Some of the services that teachers will be able to sell to businesses include communication skills, performance evaluation skills, group management abilities, and information management skills.

Schools that wish to keep their most skilled teachers will probably offer flexible work schedules so that teachers can participate in both worlds and will not be forced to make a choice. In this way, schools will not passively let businesses raid their personnel. Schools should also hunt for potential employees within the business world. Teaching teams composed of business/professional people and teachers will attract even more adults to work-study programs, as they will feel that the school knows how the business/professional world operates.

TEACHER-TEAM PERFORMANCE WILL BE REVIEWED FREQUENTLY

One objection teachers often have to proposed evaluation systems is that they rely on infrequent classroom observations for evaluation. Also, evaluators, under present systems, sometimes apply their own individual standards on how classrooms should operate.

It is now possible, however, for teachers to have their work videotaped and critiqued. It is also possible to gather information on pupil performance by computer. If teachers ignore students who are having difficulty, software programs will be able to detect how often students need help and whether they receive it. Since many students will be taught by teaching teams, the performance of teams will be evaluated as well. Since one weak teacher could reflect poorly on the whole team, there will be peer pressure for all the teachers to meet the necessary standards.

TEACHERS WILL INTERN

The teaching profession will change in yet another major way: An increasing number of prospective teachers will be placed in internship positions in school districts. During their college preparation as undergraduates, from their sophomore through their senior years, they will work as part of teacher teams in various schools. By the time future teachers finish their junior year in college, they will know whether they have chosen a field in which they can excel. This approach is already being used in many communities.

ALL STUDENTS WILL TRAIN FOR JOBS

Training for the job world does not keep people from going to college. One indication is that from 1974–1979, part-time college enrollment increased by 25.8%. More students are presently prolonging the period between when they graduate from high school and when they enter college. Some of that delay is caused by the fact that federal loans and grants for college students have declined dramatically.

As schools provide more resources for teaching adults, they will be able to offer job training based on jobs that are actually available, not those that are becoming obsolete.

From the eighth grade on, many students may actually be placed in different businesses that use the skills they are learning. If businesses that might provide a wide range of experience are not immediately available to the school, students will be able to travel to a learning center staffed with instructors and containing the latest equipment suited to students' career fields.

In either location, students will have their work supervised and graded by employers' standards. A trainer will watch them at the work site or via television hookup. (Of course, any television viewing would be with the students' knowledge and consent.) The trainer will be able to talk with the student. After this experience at the work site, students will return to the school to have their performance reviewed. The school will then judge whether the students need additional attention, practice at a simulator, or study.

Taking the last two years of high school for job preparation does not mean that the advanced-course needs of students bound for college must be put aside. Schools will, however, be forced to become more effective in teaching English, mathematics, history, and science courses before the tenth grade. Students who plan to enter professions requiring intermediate or advanced skills in foreign languages, science, or math could sample jobs in related fields while studying those subjects.

Vocational education will no longer be a narrow field of study. Rather than the quickly legislated, quickly funded, inadequate remedy for a stalled economy that it has been in the past, vocational education will prepare students for careers of challenges and changes, not just for a first job.

THE NUMBER OF HIGH SCHOOL GRADUATES WILL REMAIN CONSTANT

Presently, 33% of our population enrolls in college, but only 25% graduates. Going to college, until the early 1970s, was considered vital to career success. The economic troubles of the past decade, however, have changed this perspective.

Students who wish to attend college will benefit from an exposure to the working world and perhaps gain a better idea of what field they wish to pursue. To enter some fields requiring more advanced studies than are available in high school, students will be able to enroll in college courses geared specifically to their needs. In some cases, the necessary courses may be taught in high school.

Colleges increasingly will become the learning base for older students. Much of what is taught in graduate schools now will become part of undergraduate curricula. Faculty who wish to engage in research will be encouraged to do so and will have a job-experienced group of students to assist them.

PROBLEMS IN INNER-CITY SCHOOLS WILL INCREASE

Thus far we have described situations that will probably come to exist in all schools to a greater or lesser degree. For these schools the question is *when* adults and youth will be learning side by side, not whether it will happen. The timing and degree will depend on how quickly schools can combine the technologies of the workplace with the classroom.

For inner-city schools, however, the question is whether, not when, they will incorporate technology. If inner-city schools do not do so, their students often will have no access to technology at all. Good schools with good teachers can go for a long way toward remedying this problem. Students of the future will need schools incorporating technology to prepare them for a technological world. By the year 2000, the Census Bureau projects that 58 of the nation's cities will have a majority of minority students, many of whose primary languages are other than English. If these schools are deprived of technological aids and equipment, nearly one-quarter of our nation's youth will be unprepared to work. In addition, as we enter the 1990s, employers face the major possibility of not having enough workers for entry-level jobs. The U.S. economy cannot afford to leave one-fourth of its youth behind.

As Diane Ravitch of Columbia Teachers College has said, "Education is a forecast. We are looking at what will happen in the future so that we can decide how to prepare." We now can provide students time to create—in their communities, with their families. Communities, families, and schools together can do this in 1985. The technology is here. We can make each student's individual program of learning fit his or her own course of development. We can demand excellence, not mediocrity, from our students, our teachers, our schools.

3

TECHNOLOGY IN FUTURE SOCIETY AND FUTURE SCHOOLS

The same sociological forces that affect our society affect our schools. When the population spurts, new schools are built; when fewer babies are born, buildings are closed. If technological changes close factories in the northern states, people move to find jobs and schools open in the South.

Schools have to adapt to changes in population, national priorities, and national industries. In the last quarter century, when minorities pressed for equal recognition at the polls and in the workplace, schools reflected the resulting changes. In the future, when women press for equal recognition in legislatures and corporate boardrooms, schools will change as well. And, as Americans live longer and search for the economic means to support their longer lives, schools will change again.

Technology accelerates change in society. And today, those changes are occurring faster than ever before. Joel Goldhar, dean of the business school at the Illinois Institute of Technology, observes that "product life cycles are getting shorter. Every industry we look at seems to be undergoing shorter cycles." For example, the microcomputer, now in widespread use, was virtually unheard of 7 years ago. The refrigerator, in contrast, took more than 30 years to develop.

Technology and the changes it creates in society dramatically affect the schools. As a result, technology will soon foster a union between schools and industries from which both will profit.

BUSINESS NEEDS EDUCATION TO SURVIVE

An escalating battle between the United States and foreign countries is being fought in the electronics, aerospace, pharmaceutical, steel, agricultural, textile, and chemical industries. The United States is now competing with Japan, Korea, Taiwan, Hong Kong, Singapore, Malaysia, Brazil, and other countries where the costs of wages and many raw goods are significantly lower.

In the past, U.S. goods were competitive in the world market because of our highly educated and skilled work force, continuous innovation, and superior research and development. Throughout the 1960s, the United States was a leader in the ideas that advance technology. But our lead has been shrinking since the early 1970s. Here are some indicators:

- In 1985, the United States is still the world leader in Nobel prizes. But these prizes are the result of work begun in the late 1950s and early 1960s while federal funding was high for college-based research and development.
- More than 1 in 5 U.S. doctoral degrees in science and engineering are now awarded to foreign students. In some fields, the figures are much higher. In 1981, according to Census Bureau information, students from other countries received 52% of all American doctorates in engineering, 38% in agriculture, and 31% in computing.
- So few science and mathematics teachers now come out of college that one-third of the nation's high school students are taught science by unqualified teachers, some of whom have never had college preparation in science and mathematics.

Clearly, foreign competitors recognize the need for education in vital technological areas. If the United States is to regain its position of strength in the world economy, it will have to increase its national commitment to education.

RETRAINING

During the 1980s, many workers may not recognize the need for retraining. If they lose a manufacturing job in one city, they will be able to move somewhere else and get a similar job. They will probably have to accept lower salaries, but this will seem better than getting no paycheck at all.

By the 1990s, however, it will be clear that workers are losing jobs permanently to new equipment. Those who take the initiative to retrain themselves will find new kinds of jobs—for example, they can maintain, install, market, distribute, or modify the equipment that replaced them. But workers who do not retrain will drift to the few businesses that have not yet installed new technologies. Their ultimate fate, however, will inevitably be unemployment.

Government, unions, and businesses have all sponsored retraining programs in the past. Successes have been limited. In 1978, some employment programs were retraining union workers—for jobs as manual elevator operators or linotype operators, for both of which jobs there is little demand today, and there will be less in the future.

NEW JOBS

The need for retraining will not be confined to those who work in the manufacturing sector. Today, we can already see evidence of the kind of shifting in job responsibilities that will increase in the future. Many tasks that were formerly assigned to lawyers are now being performed by paralegals. Nurse practitioners are assuming some duties formerly undertaken by doctors.

Other changes are occurring in the workplace. Some office workers are being replaced by computers—but there is an increasing need for information analysts, communications specialists, and information storage and retrieval technicians.

The economy will not be able to accommodate, retrain, and re-employ all the displaced workers unless schools, government, businesses, and unions work and plan together. The drive to be retrained will come from individual workers, but the *place* to retrain must be provided by the leaders in government, business, labor, and education, who must see that we are competitive in a world economy.

TRAINING STUDENTS

In addition to retraining those already in the work force, schools of the future must play a more active role in preparing all students for jobs. The task will not be easy—many of the jobs students will hold during their lifetimes will not yet exist when they are in school.

Businesses can provide invaluable advice about the needs they foresee for their own workers. Today, both Chrysler and General Motors have embarked on a massive program to modernize their assembly lines, with much greater emphasis on using robots. Both companies have used public school buildings and private, company-run institutes in southeastern Michigan to provide training for interested workers and recent high school graduates. In Detroit the schools and auto industry created a preemployment academic and vocational skill assessment center. But seldom has either company gone to the municipalities where their plants are located and worked with school boards and school administrators to change the curriculum of the students *still in school* to reflect these high-technology skills.

TECHNOLOGY WILL AFFECT SCHOOLS IN OTHER WAYS

New technology will create two other major changes in the work force. Both of these changes will have a profound effect on schools. *Spin-Off Companies Will Develop.* By the late 1980s, businesses are expected to form at the rate of 700,000 firms a year. Many of these may be started by displaced workers. When office workers lose their jobs to information analysts, they may market their services to home entrepreneurs just starting their businesses. Some of today's middle managers, whose job responsibilities have been eliminated, will also be forced out of major corporations into satellite service businesses.

Not all entrepreneurs will have been forced into their own businesses. Some will be employees of large businesses who foresee little advancement in their present jobs because senior employees are neither retiring nor being promoted. As these younger employees see snags in the system, they will use their free time to develop a better-designed component, a more readily accessible information base, or a less costly way of handling the purchase of raw goods. And they will have the time to make these explorations because the efficiencies of new technology will reduce the need for personnel so dramatically that to ensure jobs for more people, the workweek will be shortened to 32 hours by the early 1990s and to 20–25 hours by the year 2000.

Companies, in turn, will encourage employees to become entrepreneurs. These self-employed consultants can frequently provide a corporation with better service at lower personnel costs. In fact, companies are already beginning to offer employees guaranteed contracts for a certain number of years to operate as consultants.

Educational programs devised by reformed school districts can help new entrepreneurs develop their businesses. Schools can teach a variety of classes specifically geared to their needs, ranging from financial planning skills for handling investments to tax laws. Entrepreneurial students will not even have to come to school to take classes—interactive cable television will permit them to study, learn skills, and even contact advisors for further information without leaving home.

Schools will also develop courses that will help younger students acquire entrepreneurial skills. Some of the entrepreneurs who were trained by the school may return to teach students the skills they have learned.

More People Will Work at Home. Many small businesses will succeed because they operate in the home—the "electronic cottage." Students, too, will be more likely to spend 1 or 2 days studying at home.

One benefit, of course, is that families will see more of each other. Parents will be more able to visit the school to talk with their children's teachers. Children will have a better idea of the kind of work their parents do.

But it is likely that these working and schooling options may become available before we have made plans to deal with their corresponding problems. For example, in a two-computer, two-salary home, when one of the computers breaks down, who will use the remaining computer? Where will family members find a quiet place to work in the home? How will children learn to become independent if parents are readily accessible?

Long ago, parents never considered that owning a telephone would eventually mean they would have to install a separate line for teen-agers. Few predicted that people would write fewer letters once they began making long-distance telephone calls. We did not anticipate that having a television in the home would mean that children would spend more hours in front of the TV than at school or in their rooms reading by themselves. Nor do we see today all the ramifications of schools of the future, which could develop into important places to get away from it all, for both adults and youth.

TECHNOLOGY IN THE SCHOOLS: THE CURRENT INSUFFICIENCY

In the early 1980s technology offered the public schools many new tools to manage curriculum, instruction, personnel, facilities, and resources. But technology is still used primarily to manage admin-istrative details. Many school districts still have only one computer per school. And in many cases, the computers that are in classrooms are used to teach computer literacy or for drill and practice.

All this will change in the future, as technology becomes more pervasive and essential. Clark Kerr, chairman of the Carnegie Council on Policy Studies in Higher Education, predicts that technology will eventually not just augment existing methods, but will actually rev-olutionize schools as we know them today. Schools will become more of a concept and less of a place.

Of course, it will first be necessary to ensure that all schools have— and use optimally—all the new technology. Studies indicate that there is still room for improvement. The 1980 National Assessment of Educational Progress determined that 75% of all classroom instruc-tion—at all levels—still comes under the broad classification of lec-turing. Audiovisual equipment is usually used only to present supplementary materials. And pocket calculators, instructional tele-vision, video cassette players, and videodiscs have frequently been unavailable to all students in the public schools.

But they are available to students at home, especially students from middle- or upper-middle-class families. According to the 1980 Cen-sus, 98% of all homes had television sets—an average of 3 in every home. Large numbers of students have their own calculators and computers at home, but do not have them at school. In samples taken in the eastern part of the United States, 90% of the parents whose income is in the upper 10% have purchased a computer, disk drive, a printer, and educational as well as business software for their homes. In contrast, only 20% of the parents whose income is in the lowest 10% have bought a computer—usually a joystick and some games.

If this trend continues, by the year 2000 this will likely be a "have" and "have-not" learning society, with a growing gulf between the two groups. Schools can help remedy this disparity. But it will require a substantial investment.

In July 1984, the North Carolina legislature voted to provide 1 computer for every 100 students in grades 7 through 12. But even this major commitment on the part of the state has meant only that each student can spend 15 minutes *each week* in computer labs. Obviously, attaining true computer literacy will require a huge investment.

In addition to increasing the technology available in schools, there will have to be a major educational effort to ensure that teachers can use it most effectively. In general, teachers are naturally most comfortable with textbooks, because that is how they were taught. Tools such as instructional television, overhead projectors, and film projectors have never achieved their full potential as teaching devices. The educational promise held out by the computer is too valuable to allow this technology to be underused.

THE PROMISE OF TECHNOLOGY

Computers and videodiscs can serve as extensions of an individual's mind to communicate information and data (text, graphics, speech, and pictures). These emerging interactive literacy technologies will include telephones, televisions, monitors, and computers that students will use for reading, writing, computing, and even drawing. And the artificial intelligence of the new computers will assist students to progress through their own individualized educational programs.

If the new learning technology is properly used, schools of the future will take on an entirely new look. The formal learning environment will not be confined to a single building. Instead, it will extend to the home, the public library, the museum, and even a college campus hundreds of miles away. Many new school buildings will be designed to coordinate with nature museums, art museums, amphitheaters, and other creative learning environments already in existence.

School buildings will change internally as areas are planned for lectures, seminars, and workshops. Viewing rooms with individual study units including computer terminals linked to mainframe computers may appear in many buildings. These facilities will be designed, moreover, to allow alterations when equipment becomes outdated.

Today, some innovative school districts have opened special schools that focus on technology. The trend toward establishing specialized technology and media schools will continue.

By 2000, computers will be available to 25% of the poorest school districts on a ratio of 1 per 8 students. In contrast, 25% of the most affluent school districts will have a ratio of 1 computer per 4 students. One-tenth of primary school students and one-quarter of secondary students may use interactive television to study at home 1 or 2 days per week.

In the year 2000, the learning environment will combine automatic and human teaching in a variety of settings to accommodate many learning styles, allow for new definitions of literacy, and foster life-long learning skills. Nine-tenths of all homes will be wired with new laser technology, and many will receive interactive cable and computer on-line networking. Students will be able to direct-dial their encyclopedias and other resources for homework, individual research, and study. The advent of this technology will make research, study, and communication skills the new basics of education.

Voice-activated computers and interactive television will change the way society evaluates schooling and what people know. Young children and handicapped learners may be able to learn and communicate more rapidly, and at higher levels of thinking and reasoning, as the more primitive means of communication take a back seat to machines that are extensions of the human mind. Nonprint will be as important as print—reading and writing may be called viewing and composing.

Acquiring the ability to find, use, and discard data, and to solve problems, will be more important than traditional research. Even students who might not succeed if taught by only traditional teaching methods will have the opportunity to become "new learners" as adults. By the year 2000, more of today's "nonachievers" may flourish as they are allowed to demonstrate their academic progress through methods other than paper-and-pencil tests. The ends of thinking and achieving in a competitive society may finally overshadow the means of achieving those ends.

Many of the details that plague administrators in 1985 will be taken over by computers. These will include: 1) scheduling, 2) attendance records, 3) payroll, 4) personnel data (certification), 5) bus scheduling, 6) cafeteria management, 7) inventory management, 8) student records, 9) budgets, 10) repair and maintenance scheduling, and 11) scheduling of extracurricular activities. As a result, administrators will have more time to concentrate on instruction and academic achievement for all students.

It is likely that educators will use computers to devise individual education plans for all students, and will use the technology available to track their progress. Data bases recording students' interests, learning styles, achievements, performance on criterion-referenced tests, demonstrated competencies, honors, awards, and other pertinent information will help schools meet individual needs.

The development of individualized or classroom-oriented learning materials by instructional design specialists and classroom teachers will lead to the improvement of educational software and courseware. Students will assist their teachers in developing or modifying existing courseware to fit their needs. Software companies will offer money to teachers, teacher-trainers, and students to develop new products. Rather than having homogeneous textbooks reflecting the publisher's idea of our nation's values, these new products will reflect the viewpoints of the authors and the regions of the country from which they came. Control Data, for example, paid teachers in 1984 to develop educational programs. In addition, educators will set criteria for better commercially developed materials using the curriculum established at the district and state level.

Textbooks may be designed as handbooks for research and study, or as guides for communication like dictionaries, grammar books, and thesauri. New handbooks on reading, writing, viewing, listening, speaking, and thinking will be developed for children, young adults, and adults. Compilations of information such as chemistry and physics books may become paper texts stored on data discs for easier updating. Courseware and textbook criteria will be compatible. More paperback textbooks will be used at the elementary and secondary levels and will be given to students to keep as part of their free public education. No single state will have a dominant influence on the national textbook market, because educators in all parts of the country will choose from a variety of instructional materials that best meet the needs of individual students.

Between now and the year 2000, the marketing of textbooks and other materials for classroom instruction will be in a transition period. Knowledge will expand at increasing rates and videodisc technology will extend the storage capability of both graphic and written material. Books will become substantially more expensive, resulting in teachers' using their own computer programs, commercial products, and student-generated programs. Parents and educators will have a variety of media from which to select materials for formal learning or leisure activities.

During the next 15 years, parents will play an important role in shaping the evolution of the educational materials that will be available by the year 2000. According to the Electronics Industry Association, about $1 billion has been spent on textbooks during the past 200 years. But by 1990, $1 billion will be spent on computer-assisted instruction, only one-third of this by the schools. The remainder will be spent by parents for home learning.

Funds for bringing the latest technology into the schools may also come from parents and concerned citizens. Parent or booster groups' fund-raising efforts may be directed at providing additional school computers. School/business partnerships, community involvement, and cooperative efforts of public schools, community colleges, private vocational schools, and private companies will supply additional funds for more education and training opportunities for adults. This situation could result in even greater disparities between large and small, rich and poor communities.

Teleconferencing will offer additional opportunities for adult training and education. Today, teleconferencing is gaining wide acceptance in business because it is often cost-effective. Millions of dollars are spent each year on adult training and education programs. Most of the money spent on such courses is for travel and per diem costs for consultants—costs that can be reduced or eliminated by tele-conferencing. One national research project conducted for a state-wide day-care training program in the South suggests that there is no significant difference between mechanical and human teaching if the information is organized similarly.

As teleconferencing opportunities increase, public school teachers will have a wide range of options available to them. They will be able to participate in superior in-service training programs to keep their professional skills continually updated. And they will be able to use their own teaching skills to develop specific programs to meet the needs of retraining or educating adult workers, who may not even be located in their own community.

CONCLUSION

Producing effective educational materials and courseware will con-tinue to be a major challenge for educators. The publishing and computer software businesses in the 21st century will change, alter, invent, and market a variety of materials for the future. Their clients are changing in both age and learning needs. Knowledge is changing and expanding overnight in many of the disciplines; home schooling is accelerating; and interactive learning centers are expanding within the private sector. School boards and administrators need to assess textbook adoption and instructional materials policies carefully to ensure that all students, present and future, will have the most rel-evant, up-to-date, and accurate learning tools and materials. Edu-cators and policy decision-makers must influence the publishing market to ensure that good materials are available.

For students, technology will be the vehicle for gathering data at their own levels of ability, according to their own learning styles. Teachers will use these modern tools for better organizing their class-rooms, learning stations, and labs, or for directing instruction through interactive computer-assisted networks. For administrators at the state and district levels, technology will be the means of streamlining education, organizing and administering data, and using teachers more efficiently and effectively.

Technology will also extend the classroom into the home, where students who need to be at home can learn uninterrupted and where individual problems can be better addressed under parents' supervision.

School administrators, parents, teachers, and students will be involved in the promotion of learning for all people and in the enhancement of all the instructional programs. Long-range planning will be essential as new learning techniques, methodologies, and human brain research evolves, for technology is a means, not an end. Imaginative leaders will be in demand to create and manage new learning environments. Technological advances will alter learning opportunities and literacy standards will extend to all the communication skills: reading, writing, speaking, listening, and viewing. With rapid development in these areas, people, the schools, and the workplace must all learn to be flexible.

4

FUTURE LIFESTYLES

Lifestyles in the future will be affected by three major changes—
shifts in demographics, changes in family patterns, and technology.
This chapter discusses each of these influences and their effect on
lifestyles in the future. Charts and tables (Figures 1 through 31) will
be found on pages 44–65.

DEMOGRAPHIC SHIFTS

A review of some of the characteristics of our future population shows
that:

- The school-age population will continue to decline in size. By
  the year 2000, only 28% of the population will be between the
  ages of 5 and 17—down from 32% in 1980 (see Figure 1).
- The median age of the population will continue to rise. It reached
  30.6 in 1982 (see Figure 2); by the year 2000, the median age
  will be 36.3.
- In 1982, about 60% of the working population was under the
  age of 40. In the year 2000, if working age is still considered
  to be between 18 and 65, only half that population will be
  under 40.
- The proportion of older Americans will continue to rise. Americans over the age of 65 presently comprise over 12% of the

population. By the year 2000, they will be closer to 17% and may compete with schools for federal funds (see Figures 3, 4, 5, and 6).

- Today's 3:2 ratio of older women compared to older men will shift. By the year 2000, as the stresses of the workplace begin to affect women's health, the margin between men and women in this 55-plus group will narrow.

- The fastest-growing group in the population will be Americans over the age of 85. Their numbers will double by the year 2000; by 2050, 1 in 20 Americans will be over 85. These Americans will have significant health, social, and economic needs, and they will not benefit substantially from the advances in medical technology, which will primarily be designed to prevent debilitation, not reverse it.

- Poverty rates among older Americans will continue to decline because more members of this group will continue to work even after "retirement" (see Figures 7 and 9).

- Poverty rates for minorities will continue to be higher than the national average. Poverty is greatest in families with a female head of household. By the year 2000, if schools provide both training for poor women and child care, poverty rates among this group may decline (see Figures 11 and 24).

- Minorities, most notably Hispanics, now make up 22% of the new entrants into the labor force. From 1990 to the year 2000, minorities figures could continue to rise (see Figures 12, 13, 14, and 15). See Figures 12, 13, and 14 for idea of numbers of minorities who will be entering the work force in the year 2000. See Figure 15 for minorities who are self-employed.

- Minorities in the year 2000 will comprise a larger voting bloc than unions (see Figures 16, 17, and 18).

- Women's political power will increase. By 2000, one of the two major parties will have a woman presidential nominee. More women will be active in politics on all levels—from city councils to the United States Senate (see Figure 19).

- Migration to the Sun Belt will continue. Americans—especially the young—will move south and west because that is where most new jobs will be created. However, small-scale businesses will be developing in the northern part of the nation.

One significant result of these demographic changes will be the increased political power that older Americans will wield in the future (see Figures 8 and 18). Older people are a major political force, voting in greater proportion to their numbers than other groups. Their political power will continue to increase into the beginning of the 21st century.

This "graying of America" will also affect the schools. There will be fewer young people to educate, and older people may not feel as much of a personal stake in continuing to support public education—unless, of course, the schools are actively involved in providing education and retraining for citizens of all ages. Illiteracy is a special concern within the 55-plus age group. Dealing with this will be an important means for schools to gain their support and to attract federal dollars (see Figure 28). Schools, as a matter of their own survival, must find ways to meet the needs of learners of all ages (see Figure 10).

The increasing numbers of minority workers—especially those whose native language is not English—will generate pressure to educate non-English-speaking workers in the language of the workplace. Additionally, we believe that businesses will ask schools to offer more foreign language instruction—not only to young people, but also to their employees who are advancing in their careers and need to communicate with business people from other countries.

Finally, the political power of women will also affect the schools. The "gender gap" is real, politically and economically (see Figure 20). Fortunately for the schools, women voters—and women office-holders—tend to place greater emphasis on issues that relate to the quality of life, and these include the schools. There will be more women school board members, city council members, and legislators determining the level of public support for the schools. More women school superintendents will represent the schools; problems of female students' access to advanced science and mathematics courses will be given more public attention.

As the population shifts even more to the Sun Belt, there will be a shortage of school facilities in those states. In other areas of the country, however, there will be a surplus of schools. School administrators in both sections of the country will have to learn to adapt to these problems. In the North and East, it is likely that at least some portion of school buildings will be rented out to businesses that provide services to the community. Day-care, for example, could be housed in unused school classrooms, enabling neighborhood schools to remain open. In the South and West, school districts may consider telecommunications as one means of handling the shortage in school facilities.

CHANGES IN THE FAMILY

More women will be employed. Almost 60% of adult women will have jobs by 1990—but the percentage of young women (ages 25 to 44) with jobs will be 70%. Many of these women will work at home for part of the week, using interactive cable television or computers with telecommunications capabilities to communicate with their offices (see Figures 22 and 23).

Fathers will be more involved with their children. Some will work at home 1 or 2 days a week, and will have more opportunity to see their children. More fathers will take some time off to stay at home following the birth of their children.

The birth rate will continue to fall. Even though minorities now have higher birth rates (2.6 births per woman of childbearing age as compared to 1.9), minority women will have fewer children as they move up the economic ladder.

Divorce rates will level off but, with longer life spans, it will not be unusual for most Americans to be divorced at least once. The effects of divorce on current family life are illustrated in Figures 24, 25, and 26.

Following a divorce, parents will most likely be granted joint custody of their children, although some custody battles undoubtedly will still exist. Divorce agreements may even specify which schools will be responsible for a child's education—a school in one part of the state may transmit instruction via cable television to another part of the state when the child is staying with the other parent.

More people will work at home. By the year 1990, 95% of all American homes will have the capability of a two-way cable system that will allow them to work at home at least part of the week. Already, most of the employees of one British computer software company are working at home, and in the United States, companies including

Control Data and Continental Illinois National Bank and Trust Company have offered some employees the option of working at home. Initially, women will be more likely than men to choose that option, especially during the years when their children are small, enabling them to continue their careers while also caring for their children. But as the year 2000 approaches, more and more men will also be working at home, at least some of the time. Spending a significant amount of extra time together will bring some families together. Others may break up as a result of the stresses of being together constantly. And when children also spend time learning at home, the potential benefits or stresses could increase dramatically.

There will be an increasing need for flexibility for working parents. By the year 2000, workers will demand such options as part-time work, flextime, and work at home.

Nontraditional families will become more usual. Based partly on economic necessity, unrelated families headed by single women may combine into a single household or grandparents may be part of a household.

The need for child care and home management will be even greater by the year 1990 or 2000. Similarly, care for aged and infirm family members will be an increasing need. In the 1990s, small entrepreneurs will provide these services. By the year 2000, some part-time workers—students, for example, or partly retired senior citizens—will establish businesses that will transport children to community service centers where other entrepreneurs will provide education or child care. Still other businesses will provide meals. Employers will offer the options of child care or parent care as an employee benefit. In some areas of the country, these service businesses may be located in underutilized school buildings.

These changes in family patterns will not mean the end of the American family. On the contrary, we believe that Americans will place more value on their families in the future, but they may define "family" differently than we do today. One of the effects of the technological revolution will be to give both fathers and mothers more time to spend with their children.

Schools will need to respond to the changing family patterns. It will be necessary for them to notify both parents, if they live apart, of a student's progress. Schools will have to adapt to shared custody arrangements and other special arrangements involving child care. During periods of family realignment, the schools will become a critical stabilizing force in children's lives. Many are already offering special counseling groups for children whose parents are divorcing; these and similar programs will be even more important in the future.

But there will also be positive benefits for the schools. As parents have fewer children, they will take a more active role in each child's education. It is even likely that parents and their children will both be attending school in the same building at least once during the child's life, since parents will be returning to school every 5 to 10 years for retraining. Communication between parents and teachers will be much more critical as each child works on an individualized education plan—fortunately, the electronic communication capabilities of the future will allow such interaction to be more flexible and comprehensive.

TECHNOLOGY

One force that will have a major social impact will be cable television. By 1986, more than half of all American households will have cable television, and these systems will provide as many as 80 subscription channels, each offering about 30 or more different programs around the clock. People will be able to enjoy cultural events in their own homes, events taking place in the next block—or around the world.

Older Americans especially will benefit from cable television. They will be able to communicate with their physicians, order their groceries, and conduct many of their other business transactions without leaving home.

Disabled citizens will also be prime beneficiaries of the new technology, because it will make it possible for them to lead self-sufficient lives. Already some companies—including Walgreen's, McDonald's, and Mountain States Telephone—are installing computer terminals in the homes of disabled people so they can work at home.

Computers will also affect most Americans' lives. Most workers will use computers on the job, and most homes will own at least one computer. Consumers will be able to book reservations for airline tickets or a favorite restaurant. They will be able to play video games against opponents who live down the block or across the country.

These interactive cable systems will make it possible to place off-track bets or check the performance of their stocks.

But computers will also allow creativity to flourish. Americans will be more likely to use computers during their leisure time to help them create with language, music, and holographic art.

And computers will also bring Americans closer to citizens of other countries by providing simultaneous translations from one language to another. Machines are already capable of recognizing the sounds and meanings of more than 6,000 words and these capabilities are increasing every day. Today, Americans receive very little news of events in other countries. In the future, they will be able to have direct access, in English, to news programs originally telecast in another country in another language.

As students and their parents use the new technology to learn more about other countries, schools will increase the amount of time spent teaching students about other cultures. And although simultaneous translating machines will be available, they will not be applicable to all situations—for example, business meetings with representatives from emerging nations, those whose languages are not yet in translation. So schools will continue to teach foreign languages to an increasing number of students. As businesses become more international, and as companies deal more and more with foreign markets, they will want to hire employees who can speak at least one other language.

As Walt Kelly's Pogo once said, as a result of these major lifestyle changes, "It seems that we are now confronted with a number of insurmountable opportunities." And the schools will be directly and significantly affected by each of these changes.

How will the new technology affect the schools? How is it possible that students will spend more time studying—but less time in school? How will these changes affect teachers? What kinds of people will be hired to teach in the schools? How will schools make sure they have the skills they need to take advantage of the new technology?

In the next several chapters, we have identified a number of specific influences and the effects they will have on the schools in the future.

Age of Groups as Share of Total Population

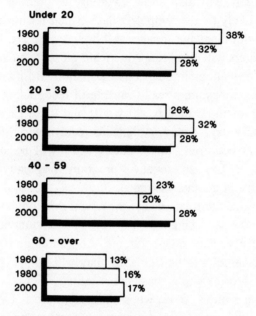

Source: U.S. News & World Report, March 19, 1984

Of the people in the 60 and over group, the fastest growing age group is age 80 and over. These people also have the most debilitating diseases and are more likely to be women.

Figure 1

Median Age in 1982
by Race and Age

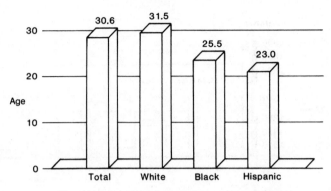

Minorities are younger than the majority population.

Figure 2

People 65 and Over: 1983

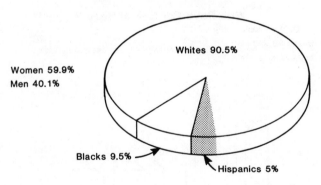

Figure 3

Population 55 and Over by Race: 1980

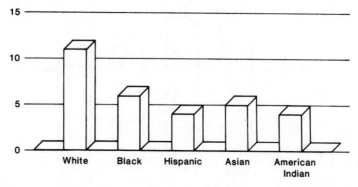

The proportion of elderly Americans has tripled since 1900. It is projected that by the year 2000, more than 20 percent of all Americans will be 55 years old and over.

Figure 4

Who Pays For Social Security

The number of people holding jobs per each beneficiary.

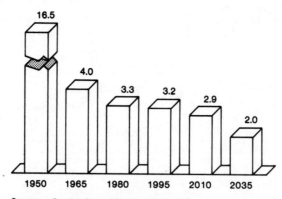

Source: Social Security Administration

Figure 6

Population 55 Years Old and Over, by Age and Sex: 1982

(in millions)

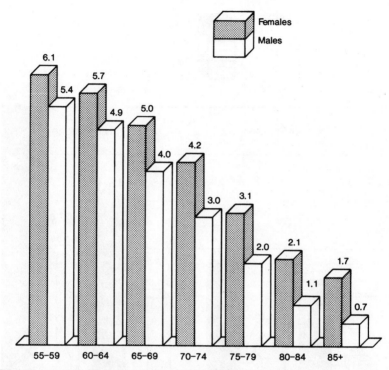

Elderly women outnumber men 3 to 2. Because the life expectancy of men is shorter than that of women, the health, social, and economic problems of the elderly are the problems of women.

Figure 5

Poverty Rate of Persons 60 and Over, by Living Arrangements, Sex, and Race:1981

Black

White

Total

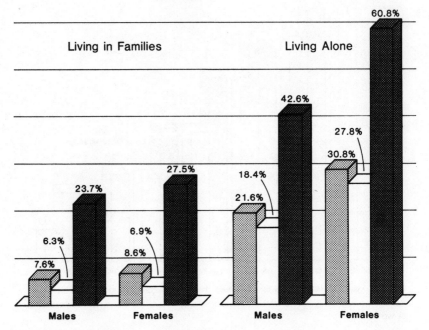

Living in Families   Living Alone

60.8%

42.6%

27.8%

30.8%

27.5%

18.4%

23.7%

21.6%

6.9%

6.3%

8.6%

7.6%

Males   Females   Males   Females

Source: Population Profile of the U.S.: 1982.
Poverty rates are high among the elderly living alone.

Figure 7

Profile of the Voter Turnout Rates of

Those Who Reported Having Voted in November 1980

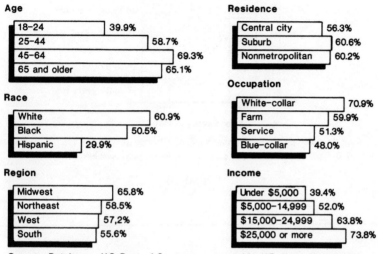

Age

18–24	39.9%
25–44	58.7%
45–64	69.3%
65 and older	65.1%

Race

White	60.9%
Black	50.5%
Hispanic	29.9%

Region

Midwest	65.8%
Northeast	58.5%
West	57,2%
South	55.6%

Residence

Central city	56.3%
Suburb	60.6%
Nonmetropolitan	60.2%

Occupation

White–collar	70.9%
Farm	59.9%
Service	51.3%
Blue–collar	48.0%

Income

Under $5,000	39.4%
$5,000–14,999	52.0%
$15,000–24,999	63.8%
$25,000 or more	73.8%

Source: Database – U.S. Dept. of Commerce, prepared by U.S. News & World Report, July 16, 1984.

Figure 8

Income of People Over 65, 1970 - 1980

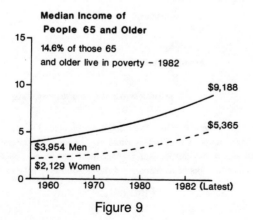

Median Income of People 65 and Older

14.6% of those 65 and older live in poverty – 1982

$9,188

$5,365

$3,954 Men

$2,129 Women

1960   1970   1980   1982 (Latest)

Figure 9

Participants in Adult Education, by Age Group

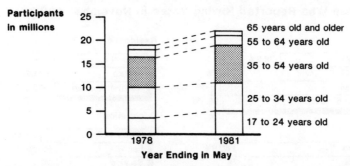

More than 21 million people participated in adult education activities in 1981, 3 million more than in 1978. Participation by all age groups grew in absolute numbers.

Figure 10

Percent of Minority Enrollment in Public Schools - 1982

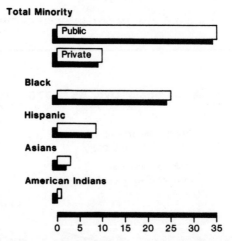

Sources: U.S. Census – Public; The Council on American Private Education.

Forecasting International feels that fertility rates may change with economic mobility, and private school enrollments may change with technological advances in public schools. Therefore, we feel that to make projections for 1990 – 2000 may be misleading.

Figure 12

Percentage of People Below Poverty Level:

By Race or Ethnic Origin: 1969, 1979, 1981, 1984

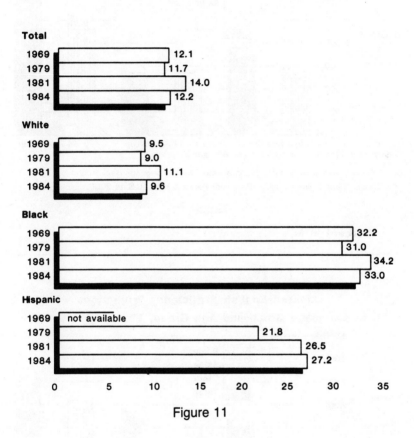

Figure 11

Limited-English-Proficiency Projections
by Language Group and Age Group, 2000 (Ages 5-14)

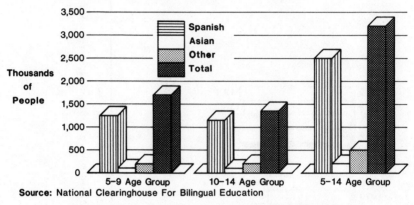

Source: National Clearinghouse For Bilingual Education

Demographic Projections of Non-English Language Background
and Limited-English-Proficient Persons in the U.S. to 2000.

Figure 13

Limited-English-Proficiency Projections
by Language Group and Age Group, 1990 (Ages 5-14)

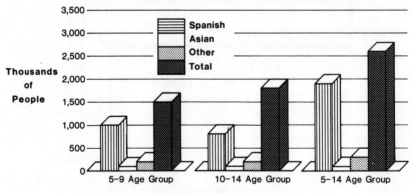

Source: National Clearinghouse For Bilingual Education

Demographic Projections of Non-English Language Background
and Limited-English-Proficient People in the U.S. to 1990.

Figure 14

Minority-Owned Firms – Summary by Industry: 1977

[These data were developed from administrative records of government agencies, various published and unpublished sources, a direct mail canvass, and personal contacts with community and government representatives knowledgeable in this area. **Caution** should be exercised in comparing data presented here with published or unpublished data from other reports of the 1977 economic censuses. Factors affecting comparability of data among censuses are scope of survey, business unit canvassed, and receipt-size limitations. See source for further detail.]

Ownership and Industry	All Firms		Firms with Paid Employees				Firms without Paid Employees	
	Total (1,000)	Gross receipts (mil. dol.)	Total (1,000)	Employee¹ (1,000)	Annual payroll (mil. dol.)	Gross receipts (mil. dol.)	Total (1,000)	Gross receipts (mil. dol.)
All industries²	**561**	**26,382**	**105**	**499**	**3,358**	**18,996**	**456**	**7,386**
Black-owned	231	8,645	40	164	1,135	6,397	191	2,248
Spanish-origin	219	10,417	41	206	1,350	7,140	178	3,277
Construction	52	2,361	12	45	396	1,613	40	747
Manufacturing	13	1,959	6	60	447	1,842	7	117
Transp. and public utilities	37	1,060	4	15	139	556	33	504
Wholesale trade	9	2,031	2	14	152	1,788	7	242
Retail trade	147	10,629	38	183	929	7,820	110	2,809
Finance and insurance³	28	1,334	3	24	212	1,043	26	291
Selected services	234	6,202	38	151	1,020	4,039	196	2,163

¹For week including March 12. ²Includes others not shown separately. ³Includes real estate.

Source: U.S. Bureau of the Census, 1977 Survey of Minority-Owned Business Enterprises, MB77-1, MB77-2, MB77-3, and MB77-4.

These figures represent the available data published in the 1983 U.S. Census Bureau publications. For women, the data was not broken up by race.

Figure 15

A Comparison between Hispanic
and Non-Hispanic Voters, 1972–1980

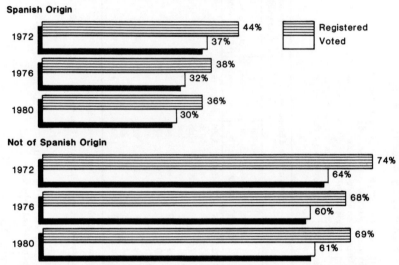

Spanish Origin

1972 — 44% Registered / 37% Voted

1976 — 38% / 32%

1980 — 36% / 30%

Not of Spanish Origin

1972 — 74% / 64%

1976 — 68% / 60%

1980 — 69% / 61%

Base–People 18 years old and over of Spanish origin or not of Spanish origin.

In each election year, voter registration and participation were lower for Hispanics than for the general population. Of the estimated 14–16 million Hispanics, only one-third are eligible to vote; large numbers are not citizens.

Figure 16

Distribution of the Spanish
Population by State: 1980

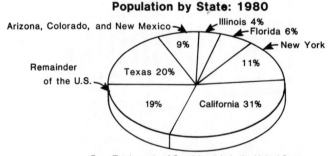

Arizona, Colorado, and New Mexico → 9%

Illinois 4%
Florida 6%
New York 11%

Remainder of the U.S. → Texas 20%

19%

California 31%

Base-Total people of Spanish origin in the United States.

These states account for 148 of the electoral votes in the U.S. Hispanics could become a voting bloc in these states.

Figure 17

Voting Blocs – Can a Candidate Pile Them Up?
People Age 18 or Older
(in millions)

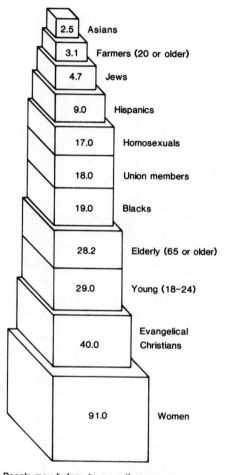

2.5	Asians
3.1	Farmers (20 or older)
4.7	Jews
9.0	Hispanics
17.0	Homosexuals
18.0	Union members
19.0	Blacks
28.2	Elderly (65 or older)
29.0	Young (18–24)
40.0	Evangelical Christians
91.0	Women

Note: People may belong to more than one group.

Source: Data base U.S. Depts. of Commerce and Labor,
US News & World Report, July 16, 1984

Figure 18

Number of Women in State Legislatures: 1983

State	Women legislators	Total legislators	Percent
Alabama	6	140	4.2
Alaska	8	60	13.3
Arizona	19	90	21.1
Arkansas	7	135	5.1
California	14	120	11.6
Colorado	25	100	25.0
Connecticut	44	187	23.5
Delaware	10	62	16.1
Florida	28	160	17.5
Georgia	19	236	8.1
Hawaii	17	76	22.3
Idaho	16	105	15.2
Illinois	27	177	15.2
Indiana	18	150	12.0
Iowa	17	150	11.3
Kansas	24	165	14.5
Kentucky	10	138	7.2
Louisiana	3	144	2.0
Maine	41	184	22.2
Maryland	37	188	19.1
Massachusetts	27	200	13.0
Michigan	16	148	10.8
Minnesota	28	201	13.9
Mississippi	3	174	1.7
Missouri	25	197	12.6
Montana	19	150	12.6
Nebraska	6	49	12.2
Nevada	6	63	9.5
New Hampshire	121	424	28.5
New Jersey	10	120	8.3
New Mexico	9	112	8.0
New York	23	211	10.4
North Carolina	24	170	14.1
North Dakota	19	159	11.9
Ohio	12	132	9.0
Oklahoma	12	149	8.0
Oregon	20	90	22.2
Pennsylvania	10	253	4.0
Rhode Island	19	150	12.6
South Carolina	12	170	7.0
South Dakota	14	105	13.3
Tennessee	9	132	6.8
Texas	13	181	7.1
Utah	9	104	8.6
Vermont	34	180	18.8
Virginia	13	140	9.2
Washington	28	147	19.0

Figure 19

Number of Women in State Legislatures: 1983 (Cont.)

State	Women legislators	Total legislators	Percent
West Virginia	17	134	12.6
Wisconsin	25	132	18.9
Wyoming	22	94	23.4
Total *	995	7,438	13.0

*Total women includes those already holding seats and those elected
in November 1982
Source: National Women's Political Caucus

Figure 19 *(cont.)*

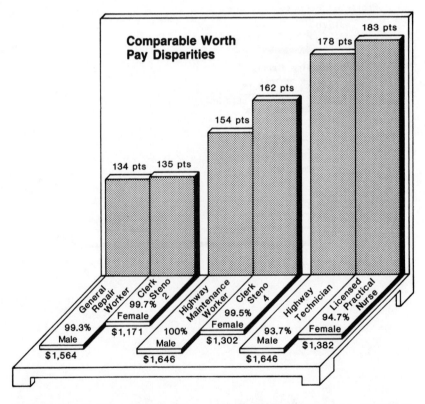

Minnesota Job Ratings revealed wide gaps in male-female pay scales for positions of comparable worth. Shaded blocks represent management consulting firms ratings of position's relative worth; outlined blocks represent actual monthly pay rates in 1979.

Figure 20

Changes in the Percentage of Women in Major Occupations Between 1970 and 1980

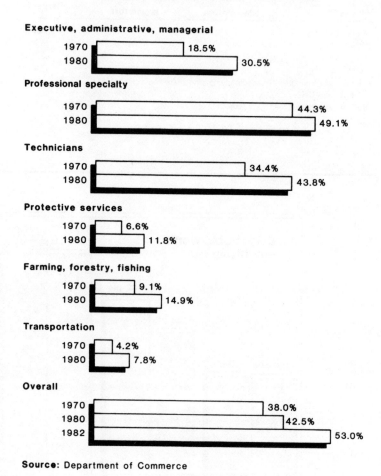

Executive, administrative, managerial

1970 — 18.5%
1980 — 30.5%

Professional specialty

1970 — 44.3%
1980 — 49.1%

Technicians

1970 — 34.4%
1980 — 43.8%

Protective services

1970 — 6.6%
1980 — 11.8%

Farming, forestry, fishing

1970 — 9.1%
1980 — 14.9%

Transportation

1970 — 4.2%
1980 — 7.8%

Overall

1970 — 38.0%
1980 — 42.5%
1982 — 53.0%

Source: Department of Commerce

Figure 21

Total Self-Employed
(in millions)*

Ten years ago, for every business owned by a woman, there were almost three owned by men. Today that gap has narrowed to a little more than 2 to 1. Here's what has happened since 1974:

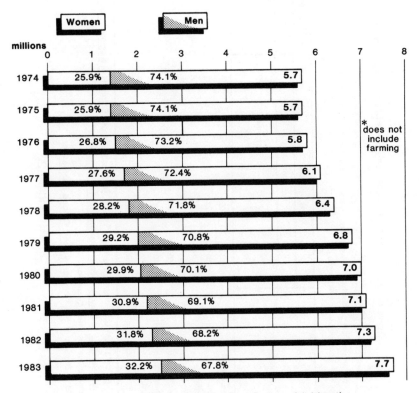

*does not include farming

Source: The State of Small Business, the Small Business Administration

Figure 22

Women-Owned Firms—Number and Receipts, by Industry: 1977

[A firm is considered to be women-owned if one-half or more of the partners are women; a corporation is classified as women-owned if 50 percent or more of the stock is owned by women. The same majority ownership criteria applies to minority-owned businesses. For coverage detail, see source.]

Industry	Firms, 1977 (1,000)			Receipts, 1977 (bil. dol.)		
	All firms¹	Women-owned		All firms¹	Women-owned	
		Number of firms	Percent of all firms		Receipts	Percent of all firms
All industries, total	9,833	702	7.1	633.1	41.5	6.6
Construction	1,107	21	1.9	72.6	2.9	4.0
Manufacturing	287	19	6.6	38.5	3.6	9.4
Transportation and public utilities	419	12	2.9	22.8	1.3	5.7
Wholesale and retail trade	2,600	228	8.8	291.4	23.4	8.0
Finance, insurance, real estate	1,404	66	4.7	66.6	2.1	3.2
Selected services	3,623	316	8.7	120.1	7.1	5.9
Other industries²	393	40	10.2	21.2	1.2	5.7

¹Based on data from U.S. Internal Revenue Service, preliminary report, Statistics of Income, Business Income Tax Returns: 1977 and Statistics of Income, Corporation Income Tax Returns: 1976.
²Includes industries not classified.

Source: U.S. Bureau of the Census, Women-Owned Businesses, 1977.

Figure 23

Families Maintained by Women:
Percent of Families

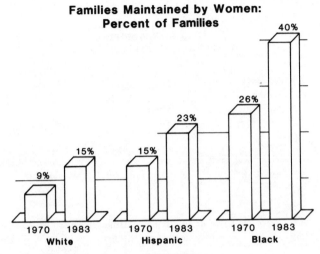

1970	1983	1970	1983	1970	1983
White		Hispanic		Black	

Source: U.S. Census Bureau, 1970/1984

Figure 24

Child Care for U.S. Preschoolers

1982 Figures

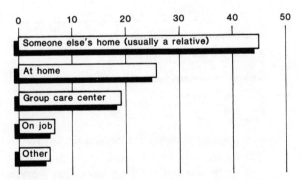

Three-quarters of all preschool-age children are cared for outside the home. In the future, business may turn to the schools to provide child care.

Figure 25

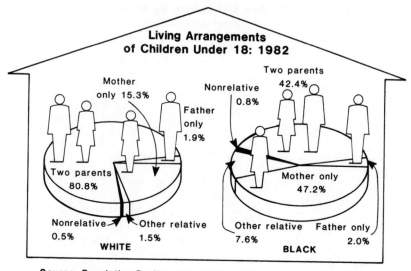

Source: Population Profile of the U.S.: 1982, Bureau of the Census.

Figure 26

Public Education Expenditures, By Source of Funds
1981 - 1984

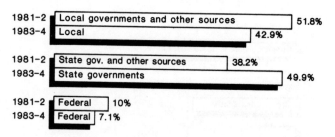

Source: Education Commission of the Schools.

1981-2 estimates – U.S. Department of Education
1983-4 – National Averages. The states do vary widely, but
the trend is definitely moving toward states being the major
source of school district funding.

Figure 27

Public Attitudes on Educational Quality
Percent by Age

The question: "Is the quality of public education better or worse than when you went to school?"

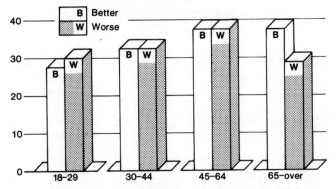

Source: The New York Times Poll, Feb. 7, 1983. Total sample indicates respondents are evenly divided – 36% – 36%.

Figure 28

Public School Support

What would guarantee a strong America?

Strong education system	88%
Strong industrial system	66%
Strong Military	47%

If more federal money were available, where would you spend it?

Public schools	21%
Health care	19%
Welfare	16%
Military	14%

How should school districts respond to budget crunches?

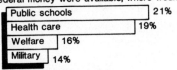

Cut teachers' salaries	17%
Don't cut teachers' salaries	76%

Source: Phi Delta Kappan, Dec. 1982. Data base – Gallup Poll, 1982 – 83 School year data for previous three years indicates continuing support for public school education.

Figure 29

The Sad State of School Plants

These 20 school districts say
they need this much more money
to repair and renovate their
school buildings.

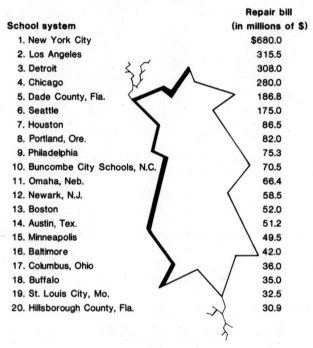

School system	Repair bill (in millions of $)
1. New York City	$680.0
2. Los Angeles	315.5
3. Detroit	308.0
4. Chicago	280.0
5. Dade County, Fla.	186.8
6. Seattle	175.0
7. Houston	86.5
8. Portland, Ore.	82.0
9. Philadelphia	75.3
10. Buncombe City Schools, N.C.	70.5
11. Omaha, Neb.	66.4
12. Newark, N.J.	58.5
13. Boston	52.0
14. Austin, Tex.	51.2
15. Minneapolis	49.5
16. Baltimore	42.0
17. Columbus, Ohio	36.0
18. Buffalo	35.0
19. St. Louis City, Mo.	32.5
20. Hillsborough County, Fla.	30.9

Source: American Association of School Administrators

Figure 30

Employer Nominations of Skills Lacked by Recent High School Graduates or Dropouts Which Cause Them to Lose Their Jobs or To Be Unsuccessful After They Are Hired

(Employers: Personnel Officers)*

Question: What are the three competencies or job preparation skills whose lack causes recent high school graduates or dropouts to lose their jobs or to be unsuccessful in their employment after they are hired?

	First		Second		Third		Total
Competencies/Skills	N	(%)	N	(%)	N	(%)	N
Work with others, settle differences	21	(5%)	12	(3%)	24	(5%)	57
Willing to improve job skills, advance	6	(1)	5	(1)	7	(2)	18
General attitudes toward work	69	(15)	61	(13)	44	(9)	174
Understands value/importance of work	12	(3)	18	(4)	23	(5)	53
Mathematics	4	(1)	1	(a)#	1	(a)#	6
Reading	0	(0)	2	(.5)	0	(0)	2
Writing	0	(0)	1	(a)#	1	(a)#	2
Speaking well enough to be understood	0	(0)	3	(.5)	1	(a)#	4
Listening well enough to understand	3	(.5)	5	(1)	6	(1)	14
Spelling, grammar	2	(.5)	0	(0)	1	(a)#	3
Use of tools & equipment	2	(.5)	3	(.5)	5	(1)	10
Quantity of work, amount of output	16	(3)	56	(12)	41	(9)	113
Quality of work, accuracy, no waste	24	(5)	55	(12)	52	(11)	131
Accepting advice and supervision	13	(3)	32	(7)	50	(11)	95
Following through on assignments	7	(2)	26	(6)	20	(4)	53
Initiative, plans, directs own work	12	(3)	18	(4)	15	(3)	45
Work habits, on time, dependable	192	(41)	58	(12)	41	(9)	291
General knowledge of business operations	1	(a)#	3	(.5)	4	(1)	8
Recognizing, solving problems by self	6	(1)	7	(2)	11	(2)	24
Making decisions in own area of work	0	(0)	5	(1)	7	(2)	12
Understands U.S. economic system	0	(0)	1	(a)#	1	(a)#	2
Applying & interviewing for a job	0	(0)	0	(0)	0	(0)	0
Personal health (avoiding illness, etc.)	2	(.5)	4	(1)	2	(.5)	8
Good appearance (grooming, dress)	1	(a)#	1	(a)#	1	(a)#	3
Safety conscious	0	(0)	3	(.5)	6	(1)	9
Flexible	1	(a)#	3	(.5)	2	(.5)	6
Specific skills required to perform job	6	(1)	4	(1)	9	(2)	19
Applying job skills to new situations	2	(.5)	5	(1)	3	(.5)	10
Understands career ladders, advancement	1	(a)#	0	(0)	0	(0)	1
Other (Specify)	3	(.5)	1	(a)#	0	(0)	4
No Response	64	(14)	77	(16)	92	(20)	659
Total	470	(101)··	470	(100)	470	(99.5)··	1836

* Employer Form A-2 respondents: 54% were personnel officers or personnel managers.

N number of responses

(a)# = less than ½%

·· Total does not equal 100% due to rounding

Source: Business and Education Survey. Parker Project—Wisconsin 1983.

Figure 31

5

21ST-CENTURY WOMEN, FAMILIES, AND THE SCHOOLS

DEMOGRAPHIC CHANGES

From the 1980s on into the 21st century, there will be more women than men in the U.S. population. More women than men will attend college, enter the work force, and start their own businesses. In 1980 women comprised 42.7% of the work force; in 1985, the figure will be 48%. And with more than 1 million women entering the marketplace each year, by 1990 the majority of America's workers will probably be women.

Businesses, families, and schools will be facing major changes. To understand some of these changes, we can study women who have graduated from college since the mid-1960s. By 1979, 67% of this group of college graduates entered the labor force, making it the largest group of first-time female entrants ever. This same group, aged 20–44, has generally delayed having children—waiting until an average age of 37 according to some studies.

More women than ever are obtaining advanced degrees and breaking into professional fields once considered the male's domain. A record number became lawyers, doctors, ministers, architects, construction workers, and computer operators during the 1970s. In 1971, women made up 758 of the 21,417 students enrolled in graduate business schools and only 3.5% of the Master of Business Administration (MBA) candidates. A decade later, there were 14,500 female MBA candidates, or 26% of the total. In the late 1960s, male law students outnumbered women 23:1. By the mid-1980s, women comprised 34% of the total.

ECONOMIC AND SOCIAL CHANGES

The composition of the work force may change from economic pressures. The traditional question for women of this century—to work or not to work—may not even exist in the 21st century. Most women will have to work so that their families will have enough money. Technological advances will allow businesses to reduce the number of hours employees work and the number of employees required to do a job. Fewer workers will be producing the same number or an even greater number of goods than was possible in the previous decade. Thus, two incomes will usually be necessary to provide most educational advantages, leisure activities, and upward social mobility, as well as food, clothing, and shelter.

This trend will bring changes to every segment of our society. Businesses will have to supply child care, assist the spouses of new employees in locating jobs, and provide flexible work hours for both men and women who need to tend their children. Families may hire teenagers, immigrants, or older citizens to provide the services formerly handled by the homemaker, or they may recruit grandparents or recently divorced relatives to live with them. Schools will no longer be able to rely so heavily on women for some volunteer services. They may turn instead to retired or partially retired people to tutor students, provide clerical support, run bake sales, and assist in the library.

Women will continue to enter professional fields in greater numbers, may not interrupt their careers for childrearing, and will have more influence on policymakers in government and business because they will be wealthier, hold more powerful positions, and be more numerous than before.

Another group of women will have more influence, not because of their wealth, but because of their poverty. In the early 1980s, 1 in every 7 families was headed by a woman—up from 1 in 10 families in 1960—and roughly 40% of these families were below the poverty line, 55% of those with children. These women will also expect day-care to be available. In the future, the woman heading a family whose income is below the poverty level may receive day-care assistance from government programs in schools that may also be training her for a new job.

DEMAND FOR DAY-CARE AND THE ROLE OF THE SCHOOLS

The first educational facilities to offer combined job training and day-care programs could be private vocational schools and community colleges. But as businesses become more involved in legislated training programs, they will turn to public schools as the most economical and widespread providers of services. Schools, after all, understand child development. Beginning in 1995, the growing numbers of workers in what have been traditionally women's jobs—nurses, school teachers, secretaries, and retail clerks—will have the advantage of day-care.

Businesses with day-care? Two changes will bring this about. The first will be a labor shortage in the new high-technology positions associated with computer operation, maintenance, and quality control. These positions will initially be more attractive to women than to men: Although the salaries may seem relatively high to many women, they may seem relatively low to most men. Businesses will also attract women to training programs by offering, as fringe benefits, day-care for children and for older relatives living at home.

The second change will occur in what has been considered the traditional women's fields. Some will disappear. Many office workers will be replaced by computers, managed by information specialists. Some former office workers will become technicians. Other job areas frequently held by women, such as those in health-care services or telemarketing, will grow so quickly that they too will suffer labor shortages. To attract workers, both male and female, wages will need to be increased and day-care services provided.

Public schools will be the beneficiaries of these job-market changes, selling day-care services in conjunction with training programs. Care must be taken to ensure that this service is available to people of all income levels. As a service to business, schools may consult on the development of day-care programs or offer them on a contract basis.

CHANGES IN THE HOME AND IN THE FAMILY

In 1983, more than 55% of all women between 25 and 44 years of age worked outside the home. By 1990, 85% of all women in this age group will be working, 65% of them full-time. With so many women working, men and women will have to readjust household duties. Before the workweek declines to a 32-hour average in 1990, most families will try to purchase household services: fast-preparation meals, part-time housekeeper/nannies, lawnmowing, and tutoring. By the mid-1990s, men of the house will share even more household duties simply because they will often be home when women are at work.

CHANGES IN THE FAMILY— ROLE OF THE PUBLIC SCHOOLS

To lessen the traumatic effect divorce has on children, divorce settlements in the future may include more balanced custody arrangements. Children could attend 2 schools with entirely different social settings. For example, in an area where mothers are predominantly executives and professionals, children will have to become independent earlier in their lives. In other areas, more mothers may be job-sharing or working part time. These different styles of parenting will teach children leadership and teamwork skills that will carry over into their school experiences and, eventually, the workplace.

Children will be able to take whatever leadership and teamwork skills they have learned at home and focus them, alone or in teams, on solving problems in various subject areas, an activity that teachers of the future will use more often in connection with computers. Teams of students will be able to solve problems. Of course, mathematics and science will be fertile ground for problem-solving, but language, history, and the arts will provide opportunities as well. Primarily, this will be done through simulation. Students will be able to take on the role of a muckraker in American literature, or a Civil War general, or a composer using the pentatonic scale. Girls and boys will learn where they have strengths as information-gatherers and where they have strengths as group leaders. Both will learn where they excel as well as where their weaknesses lie.

SCHOOL AS FAMILY CENTER

If families are having difficulty in adjusting to the stresses of 2 careers or recent second marriages, they will be able to turn to the school. Cable television courses and courses provided through the school video library could help. Schools might also serve as satellite counseling centers or recreation centers for the families facing stress.

In fact, the school of the future will be able to use the time before and after the academic day to offer a wide variety of family services. Private entrepreneurs and public agencies, renting space in the schools, may provide transportation for senior citizens and families on welfare. Nutrition services located in school buildings may ensure that fast foods are available for the teenager, hot meals for the older family member, and special diets for the infant, the ambulatory patient, or the diabetic. Telemarketing stations, computer terminals operating like electronic mail-order catalogs, may also be available for the working parent.

Public health agencies have already found that some of the most effective programs for preventing or dealing with teenage pregnancies, for working on suicide prevention, drug rehabilitation, and drug abuse are located in the schools, which serve as satellite centers. Special programs may be available either in large centers located in a school itself or through communication hookups placed in the school. It will be possible, for example, for medical personnel to diagnose pregnancies or drug abuse problems via interactive television. Once the student's condition has been determined, he or she may obtain a sense of direction and immediate goals through similar means.

SCHOOLS AS NEIGHBORHOOD EMPLOYERS AND EMPLOYMENT AGENCIES

Schools of the 1990s will be dealing not only with alienated youth but with adults who feel separated from the rewards of our society. Women who are not working may be part of this alienated group. A report published in 1984 by the University of Michigan shows that working is an important factor in self-esteem. Working single women, according to the report, have the highest self-esteem, working married women the next highest. The single working mother often has lower self-esteem, but, according to the study, many women homemakers with children have the lowest self-esteem, despite the importance of their roles. Schools may be in a position to address the needs of women who are not working outside the family—women who may feel increasingly alienated from society as they see that they are part of a smaller and smaller group. Schools can help them by employing them to run day-care centers, geriatric programs, services connected with neighborhood learning centers, or services compiling data bases, working on flexible time schedules from their homes or neighborhoods.

Schools will also be natural locations for data banks detailing the labor needs and supply of each community. Some schools may become satellite employment offices, serving local government, businesses, and private individuals. Both the adult going through regular retraining every 5 to 10 years and the high school student going through his or her initial job internship may be able to turn to the school for information about job placement. A career counselor will review an applicant's employment history and match it against the needs of the immediate community. In fact, employment services in different schools may very well communicate with each other to determine whether job placement is available in a nearby community or across the country. These services will be valuable tools for businesses transferring an employee or assisting an employee's spouse to find a new job. Schools will become more like businesses before and after the traditional academic day as the role of women in the workplace changes, for they will have space and staff to provide training programs, day-care service, counseling services, job-placement programs, and entertainment centers. Schools, however, will often have to charge for these extended-day services. In most cases they will be nearly self-supporting.

IMPLICATIONS

- As more and more women enter the work force, day-care will be in greater demand and schools will be in a position to provide it.
- Schools will play a major role in holding families together by providing day-care, geriatric care, employment for homemakers, and recreation for community residents.
- Schools' volunteer programs will depend more and more upon the elderly, as women enter the job market in greater numbers.
- Communities and states must make it possible for schools to boost pay to attract qualified people to the schools and keep the ones they have, since many other career opportunities will be open.
- Schools and communities need to take the lead in changing attitudes about the potential of women in society and in providing services such as day-care that will help women advance.
- Schools increasingly must offer services for students from homes in which both parents work (latchkey children).
- Schools must become more flexible in setting times for parent-teacher conferences and in holding various types of meetings involving parents and the community.
- Communities will need to determine the appropriate roles for the schools and other institutions in dealing with the changing status of women.

6

MINORITIES AND SCHOOLS OF THE FUTURE

As a result of the War on Poverty and the civil rights movement, disadvantaged students during the past 2 decades have been receiving special federal funds for intensive help in basic reading and mathematics. These funds will probably continue into the mid-1990s, although legislation may encourage greater private-sector involvement, particularly at the high school level.

According to the Social Security Administration's 1980 figures, 11% of whites, 34% of blacks, 28% of American Indians, 20% of Hispanics (but almost 35% of mainland Puerto Ricans), and 12% of Asians in the United States are poverty stricken.

All in all, minorities composed nearly 23% of our population in 1980. By the year 2000, they will compose 29% of the population. Even with imprecise figures, census data show that minorities are poorer than whites; they are less educated and have higher rates of unemployment.

MINORITIES AND EDUCATION

Although both blacks and Hispanics have made educational gains since the 1970 census, as a group they are still behind the white population. Of the total U.S. population, 88% graduated from high school. Of Hispanics overall, 58% graduated, with Cubans representing the greatest attainment at 71%. Nearly 55% of blacks graduated from high school, more than double their 25% rate in the 1950s.

The dropout rate of minorities will continue to decline. When schools implement the necessary programs to make sure all students have a better chance at meeting the new, higher standards that now exist in many school systems, the results will look quite promising. For example, Boston has made a contract with its high technology companies to provide job slots to all high school graduates in certain target schools—*if* the students meet performance standards.

Having computers maintain school records may help students meet these standards. If schools can place students in job internships, they can use computers to monitor both school instruction and on-the-job performance. From this information, prospective employers will be able to get an indication of how well a student performs. Computers will also be able to monitor the promptness with which students meet their assignments, the contribution of one student to the efforts of a working team, and the times students look for additional responsibility on their own.

This is precisely the kind of information that employers value. Surveys in 1983 have shown that a majority of employers prize responsibility, willingness to accept direction, and cooperation more than academic achievement. Employers will have access to both academic qualifications and job performance data of a student's ability. This should help minority students overcome some employers' biases against hiring employees from nonintegrated, inner-city schools.

Contracts between businesses and schools will become more common if federal legislation provides incentives for private-sector participation. Sources at the U.S. Department of Education indicate that federal funding for such incentives is projected to increase until the end of the century.

Still, federal funding to date has been insufficient to counter high unemployment among minorities. The unemployment rates for whites went from 5% in 1973 to 8.6% in 1983, but has decreased since then. The minority unemployment rate has continued to increase. The unemployment rate for blacks was 20.6% in 1984 and 14% for Hispanics. If federal funding is not high enough to reverse this trend, businesses will need to shoulder more responsibility than they have in the past.

MINORITIES AND POLITICAL POWER

The impact on the schools of the continuing civil rights efforts of various minority groups will most probably result in an increase of job-training programs for minorities. Local officeholders and candidates for office can help inform their minority-group constituencies of community-wide job opportunities as a way of maintaining the candidate's power base. The political power of minority groups will also become visible in school/business partnership negotiations.

MINORITY PROGRAMS STRATEGIES WILL IMPROVE GENERAL EDUCATION

Special programs for disadvantaged students have provided a great deal of information about learning problems. The research on effective schools that started at the end of the sixties and lasted for 10 years used students from special programs for many studies. Much of what is known about students whose first language is other than English has come from bilingual education research funds. Special education programs for the handicapped and for those with emotional problems have contributed to a system that will be used increasingly in the future—the Individual Education Plan.

In the future, successful strategies from the special federally funded programs for education will be used in general education. Some of the ways are as follows:

- An estimated 400,000 job slots for U.S. companies operating in foreign countries are lost each year for Americans overseas because they cannot speak the local language. Some need another language to be employed by foreign firms operating in the United States. Successful bilingual education strategies will be used in general foreign language instruction by the mid-1990s.
- The means to drill, correct, and provide listening practice in foreign languages through computer-controlled videodiscs will become more commonplace. "Ham" computer communication networks will assist language learners to perceive and make use of the subtle social differences that distinguish foreign from native speakers. Language learners will spend hours with "wire pals" in other countries.

- Social anthropologists who currently assist teachers in categorically funded reading programs and in bilingual education will be used by company managers to assess the cultural patterns in their employees' communities. This will provide tools to make working environments meet employee needs.
- Public schools—with students' permission—will use the resources of the student record office and the statewide vocational education counseling systems to offer cable information to potential employers.
- Early childhood education and geriatric service centers will be operated by both public schools and private companies. The educational content of these programs will be provided by public school programs televised to the private schools and companies over interactive cable television, or private schools will be able to purchase videodiscs that can be controlled by the students themselves on their computers. Yes, three-year-olds will run computers. Additional programs will upgrade the skills of the permanent staff of these facilities. Special materials will be developed and packaged for training the part-time workers, the volunteers, and the new workers.
- Public schools will begin using other sources of funding to enter the adult retraining market; the schools will need a different sort of funding to supply the simulation equipment needed to train in such fields as robotics, housing maintenance, and medical diagnostics.
- Public schools have been part of government-funded poverty programs for school dropouts. For adults, schools will be the main source of literacy programs. Adults can work and at the same time learn the oral and written skills they need to deal with the vocabulary of that workplace. Learning diagnosticians on the school payroll will help employers analyze skills needed for entry-level workers.

IMPLICATIONS

- Immigrants from other countries will learn English and assimilate into the U.S. culture more easily as educational techniques improve.

- As blacks and other minorities gain educational and political power, tension will increase among minorities unless community planners foresee this possibility and deal with equity issues early on. The tension may spill over into schools.
- Schools will be the main providers of literacy programs for minority adults, who will be learning the oral and written skills they need in the workplace while holding down a job. Learning diagnosticians from the school will be paid by businesses to help employers analyze skills needed for entry-level workers.
- Schools must define for their communities the benefits of education for all and the high cost of neglecting education for any group.
- The federal, state, and local governments must become more responsive to the growing minority population and must ensure that high-quality education and training programs exist. Funding incentives to the private sector must continue.
- Business partnerships and other partnership efforts to deal with the educational needs of minorities will be successful only if those partners are fully committed to making it work.
- School and community planners must be vigilant in ensuring that the gains for equity made during the past two decades are not lost.

7

FUNDING

No issue confronting schools today will have as great an impact on the future of education as the question of funding. Citizens must find ways to solve the funding problems schools face today—and to increase revenue substantially—if our nation is to meet the challenges of the future.

Educational costs, which have been rising steadily since 1970, will continue to increase. Teachers' salaries must be raised, old equipment replaced. According to recent data cited by *U.S. News and World Report*, one-fifth of the nation's vocational education equipment is broken down or has been rendered obsolete by current job changes and requirements.

Old and poorly maintained schools will continue to strain budgets. In the 1970s, tight dollars led to decreasing portions of school budgets being used for school maintenance: replacing boilers, painting, replacing broken windows, and tearing down and replacing 100-year-old schools in our cities and 20-year-old, hastily constructed schools in the suburbs. As a result, the American Association of School Administrators now estimates that to bring schools up to an acceptable, usable physical condition, school maintenance budgets must be increased to 14.7% of total budgets, up from 6.7% today (see Figure 30, Future Lifestyles). That means an estimated $25 billion for deferred physical maintenance alone.

Other costs for schools will include:
- replacing teachers who will be retiring by the early 1990s—as many as 25% of those now teaching—and the new teachers who will be hired under higher wage scales;
- hiring new teachers for the "baby echo" students now entering elementary schools;
- additional secondary school teachers when these students reach high school;
- paying bonuses to retain those math and science teachers who would otherwise accept better-paying jobs in industry or business;
- educating all students in some vocational area, whether they will enter college, a technical school, or the job market after they complete high school. All students must have marketable knowledge and skills upon graduation (see Figure 31, Future Lifestyles);
- acquiring computers, telecommunication equipment, and simulators for technological education, and training and support of both the adult and adolescent students who will use this new equipment;
- absorbing private school students attracted back to the public schools because of the greater number of services they will offer;
- making school plants attractive to public agencies, professionals, and businesses that may wish to locate in schools to offer their services to the adult learners who will be attending.

SOURCES OF SUPPORT

To some extent, federal funds will help schools meet these costs in the immediate future. However, federal funds have always been a small part of total education budget. Over the past few years, federal education grants have contributed an average of 8% of local education budgets. Planners should realize that federal spending will not increase significantly in the future.

The largest source of school funds is through state budgets, which contribute nearly 50%. In most cases—even in the 21 states where local property taxes contribute the majority of school budgets—state funding still makes up nearly 40% of the total (see Figure 27, Future Lifestyles).

During the past 10 years, all states have spent more on education, but some have not increased their budgets as fast as others. In most cases, the states with the smallest increases are those that had the least to spend—for example, in "smokestack" states where formerly profitable factories have been closed.

At the end of the 1970s, many states passed property tax caps, legislation limiting the amount taxes can increase. In some states, school services were so severely cut that many schools considered closing before the end of the school year. Winning support for local school tax increases is time-consuming and often detracts from the school's focus on education for students.

The most profitable source of support for education will come from increasing the state or community's total tax base. Attracting and keeping a vital business community is essential. *INC* magazine found that five ingredients are critical in attracting business: capital resources, state policies to support business, favorable tax structures, an educated labor force, and a high level of business activity. Each is related to education.

If a state's citizens are equipped to perform jobs projected to become increasingly available in their area in the immediate future, then the state can afford to offer tax incentives, build capital resources, and emphasize business as a priority. States will be able to train their citizens for productive jobs, and will eventually be able to build or renovate business communities to enhance consumer spending.

STATE FUNDS AS THE PRIMARY SOURCE OF SCHOOL DISTRICT EQUITY

One of the hardest problems for states over the past decade has been to provide all of its citizens, rich and poor, with basic literacy skills. The first issue state planners have tried to deal with is money—how to get more money to the poorer districts. In fact, the federal courts have brought action against one-fifth of the states, ruling that the systems these states have used for distributing state educational aid did not provide educational equity. But money alone will not ensure that students succeed. Student standards, teacher standards, objective and relevant evaluation of each component of the school, and a look at what happens to students after they graduate are important as well.

Since the Constitution mandates that education is the responsibility of the states, states will need to realize that when businesses start providing funds directly to schools in sizable quantities, they will be dealing with a new situation. Businesses could help states address educational equity more effectively. They could also, however, aid some school districts to the exclusion of others and aggravate problems that already exist. State policies enforcing high standards of student and teacher performance and effective evaluation systems should make the state as a whole attractive for business investment.

Businesses have much to gain by helping all school districts achieve educational excellence; they will broaden the consumer base for their goods and services. By investigating, utilizing, and investing in all school districts, rich or poor, they will gain another vital resource— potential future employees. The U.S. Department of Labor predicts an entry-level worker shortage during the 1990s. Businesses will have a stake in assuring that all students achieve the skills necessary for employee excellence. And state governments will need to ensure that both their educational and business policies reflect the interactive nature of business and educational achievement.

Businesses consider the quality of the schools before they agree to move to a new community. Education contributes to the whole quality of life of a community, essential today in attracting and keeping businesses. So good schools are a prerequisite for business growth, which in turn stimulates a stronger economy and tax base, providing more funds for education (see Figures 28 and 29, Future Lifestyles).

It is clear, then, that money spent on education is an *investment* that a state or local government makes in its future. It will pay off not only in a better-educated population, but also in the continued health and growth of the community or state.

Both attracting business and upgrading education should be seen as a state, as well as a local problem. In some areas of the country, a regional approach may work best. Minnesota and Wisconsin, for example, have instituted a number of cooperative programs to attract new businesses to the region. And any incentive programs that states offer to businesses should include the condition that businesses and schools work together to upgrade the labor force. If all efforts are concentrated only on attracting business, the business will not remain very long. Businesses will have no one to work with them and no one to buy their goods.

Curriculum leaders need to work with business leaders to help plan educational programs for youths who will eventually enter the work force. Businesses will be able to avoid expensive retraining because workers will have been prepared for existing jobs using the latest technology and equipment. Federal funds for job training must be used hand in hand with state tax increases to make sure that businesses already in the state can afford to stay and that new businesses will be attracted there.

RETRAINING OLDER WORKERS

Schools will generate additional income by constantly retraining older workers. Thus far, neither businesses nor schools have viewed training older adults as their specific responsibility. Community colleges and universities, as well as the private vocational schools, have been the first to provide this training. If local schools have been involved, it has been mostly in renting space to the colleges and universities. In some cases, however, contracts for training have been developed. Public schools have the resources to do this training themselves and by the year 2000 more will recognize the potential of classrooms unused after 4:00 P.M. each day.

Schools can train workers in their home communities instead of asking them to travel great distances to a college campus. Public schools have enough teachers to spread out into the business community; they do not have to tie themselves to a credit-hour, a school term or semester, as colleges must. Thus, public schools can offer short-term courses. Teachers who have the skills can train a group of workers for a one-month period and then move on to another group.

Public schools are well equipped to offer the kinds of courses adults want for retraining. Adults will find it difficult to go back into a classroom, and many do not want long, information-loaded courses. In general, they will want short-term courses that will show them how to work with certain equipment or provide them with specific, essential knowledge or skills.

IMPLICATIONS

- School districts should plan to raise teachers' salaries and implement curriculum using the new technologies. If one is sacrificed for the other, these districts will not attract businesses to their communities.
- Communities will find that placing limits on taxes will not stop the need for more school funds. Lifting caps will not generate new funds. The only solution will be to create a broader, healthier tax base.
- Citizens will come to understand that high-quality education is an investment, not an expense. People who are well educated and well trained can be more easily and quickly retrained.
- School officials, school boards, state legislatures, and citizens should not depend for support on funding sources that are overly vulnerable to change, such as sales and excise taxes, but should develop other sound, adequate funding sources.
- As alternate funding sources are added, states should ensure that schools do not lose the progress they've made in equity. For example, if schools depend on business and industry for some funding, states must keep in mind that some communities are wealthier than others, some have a greater business support base than others, which could create equity problems among districts.
- Since schools are people-intensive organizations, inflation affects them even more severely than some other institutions. For example, health costs generally rise faster than other costs and health insurance for employees becomes more expensive. The cost of energy, in the past, has also escalated rapidly during time of shortage. Schools are unable to pass these costs along to the consumers in the same way businesses can. They are often forced to cover them by taking funds from instruction.
- Parents and other volunteers will be able to provide services in some areas at little or no cost.
- Funding will be required for equipment for vocational education, computers, and training of staff in a variety of areas.
- The cost of borrowing money is going up. Schools that have to sell bonds to finance improvements will have to compete with

the federal government's need for money to cover the growing national debt.

- Schools will become more entrepreneurial. For example, they will sell various educational services and perhaps even rent land owned by the school system for various purposes, in those states where this approach is possible.

8

SCHOOL/BUSINESS PARTNERSHIPS OF TODAY AND TOMORROW

Business partnerships with schools have existed from at least as far back as the 1860s when, for example, the New York City Chamber of Commerce had representatives on the school board of the Merchant Marine Technical School, a public school in the New York City system. Chamber representatives still serve on that board today.

While business cooperation with schools is not new, partnerships between businesses and schools will be a pervasive part of the daily operations in most school districts by the 21st century. Many schools will depend on businesses for a large part of their funding, staff, and equipment. In addition, many schools will use the workplace to train students in specific job skills, whether students intend to go to college or take on full-time jobs after they graduate.

Businesses will depend on schools to update the training of their current workers and provide experienced high school graduates for future employment needs. Schools and businesses will each be critical to the survival of the other.

WHAT'S HAPPENING NOW

In 1984, the U.S. Department of Education counted 46,338 business/school relationships in 4,000 (or 25%) of the nation's school districts. Many business representatives serve in community action groups. In

Gaston County, North Carolina, for example, a 1,500-member volunteer task force consisting of business representatives, school personnel, and citizens polled the county. Through the attention generated by this community forum, an astonishing 92% of those who received the survey returned it—and 59% of them said that they would be willing to pay higher taxes to support improvements in reading, mathematics, and computer courses in the public schools.

Other examples of business assistance include adopt-a-school programs, scholarship programs for students and teachers, and training programs for school administrators. They also furnish materials and equipment and loan individual staff members for extended periods of time. In Atlanta alone, 50 schools have been adopted by 103 different businesses.

In some cities in Louisiana, chemists team-teach chemistry classes, demonstrating how the experiments students are conducting are like those that professional chemists use on the job. In other cities, engineers visit math classes and develop assignments similar to those they face in their own work.

Today, more businesses aid schools than the reverse. But in the future, many schools will be able to generate funds by selling school services to businesses directly. In 1982, businesses spent nearly 60 billion dollars, 2 billion in remedial training alone. At this time, larger corporations generally rely on their own resources or turn to community colleges and universities for help. But the public schools can offer similar services at competitive prices. In Orlando, Florida, public schools train Disneyworld employees in the maintenance of their animated figures. They also provide training for the Orlando police department.

FUNDING AND PLANNING

Corporate support of education reached an estimated $1.3 billion in 1982, 20.4% more than 1981 level, according to the Conference Board, an organization representing the largest United States corporations. The manufacturing and insurance sectors gave almost .5% of pretax income to education, with engineering and construction companies contributing 41.4% of the total corporate support. Colleges received the major contributions. Exact statistics on contributions to public schools, however, are difficult to tabulate, since most school systems have no formal records for this data.

In the future, some businesses will donate monies for specific projects; others will donate up-to-date equipment so that students can be trained in the latest technologies.

A NEW PATTERN OF COMMUNITY INVOLVEMENT

In 1984, forty-six governors initiated state-level task forces for school/ business planning. Twenty-seven have started implementing their plans. More than 250 individual task forces have been examining local issues. Many of the latter groups have published reports outlining their priorities, but so far very little central planning and budgeting is taking place.

Action still seems to occur mostly at the individual school level. Local administrators, such as principals, make contacts with local businesses. They plan together; they take action together. Their planning sessions involve the communities surrounding the school.

It is important that the large state task forces and the local task forces that they spawn examine why these local schools have successful projects.

TRAINING

In the future, schools will not only look to businesses as sources of equipment and personnel on loan. They will also regard businesses as a source of income as they provide training and retraining services for businesses and their workers. If predictions hold true, by the year 2000 only 24% of the nation's population will be young people. The other 76% will be adults, prime candidates for retraining courses.

Of course, not all retraining will take place in the public schools. Some will still be a simple on-the-job procedure. But taking a look at just one job that currently involves retraining will illustrate the future trend toward more in-depth retraining in a variety of jobs.

Medical technicians today learn how to monitor machines to determine whether there are errors in the results of various lab tests. Today, they must learn to operate one machine in a one-week intensive training session. In the future, hospitals will need several machines to be monitored in the hematology lab, several in the cytology lab measuring irregularities in the skin, bone, and organ cells being examined, and several more in the quality-control labs checking organ implants. Retraining will be periodic and continuous as the machines become increasingly sophisticated. And this training will involve not only technical skills for operating the equipment but also more sophisticated levels of analysis and judgment. Public schools can do this retraining instead of the corporations that sell the machines. Schools are better located than these companies, now situated mostly on the East Coast.

Some retraining will be quite extensive because adults will be learning new jobs. When automobile factories in Michigan and Ohio laid off workers in 1974–75, technology was already changing the nature of their industry. New careers in the high-tech automobile industry will be available only to those who are willing to be retrained. Putting robots to work at GM may generate 6 jobs for each robot, but those 6 jobs may not necessarily be on the GM production line. Instead, the new openings will come in companies that produce, sell, install, repair, and service the machines—primarily in the service sector rather than in production jobs.

WHO SHOULD LEAD?

Businesses should take the initiative in forming planning groups: They know how many workers will be replaced by technology and what kinds of new jobs it will generate. But if businesses don't take the first step, schools should do so as a matter of their own survival. Without the tax base of a healthy business sector, schools will be unable to continue to grow and flourish.

As schools approach businesses to discuss cooperative arrangements, they should bear in mind that they already have a great deal to offer. They have impressive facilities for training groups of people—auditoriums, gymnasiums, cafeterias, networks of classrooms, and stores of teaching equipment. Most of all, schools have dedicated, experienced teachers and administrators whose knowledge and organizational ability could work to the advantage of the business community.

REQUIREMENTS OF THE BUSINESS COMMUNITY

Since 1983, reports from various individuals, business representatives, public school and college personnel, and government agencies have been addressing the types of training required by businesses and industry. Their questions include:

- What kind of training will be needed for youth who dropped out of school 1 year ago, 5 years ago, or 10 years ago?
- What kind of training will be needed for the functionally illiterate adults of our country?
- What kind of training will be needed for the entire labor force if skills become outdated every 5 or 10 years?

The National Academy of Science's *High Schools and the Changing Workplace* surveyed business leaders to find out the types of skills they would like to see in high school graduates. Those who responded to the survey would like to see high school graduates who are able to:

- identify problems;
- consider and evaluate possible alternative solutions, weighing their risks and benefits;
- formulate and reach decisions logically;
- separate fact from opinion;
- adjust to unanticipated situations by applying established rules and facts;
- work out new ways of handling recurring problems;
- determine what is needed to accomplish work assignments;
- understand the purpose of written material;
- verify information and evaluate the worth and objectivity of sources;
- interpret quantitative information as, for example, in tables, charts, and graphs.

The list goes on to include knowledge of particular subjects, especially the sciences. The Academy's list of skills, however, could apply to college graduates, doctoral students, and experts as well as high school students. It failed to pinpoint the degree of skill necessary in each category for high school students.

Most of the reports on business needs have not focused on entry-level and mid-level jobs or on the design of retraining programs in the future, and are therefore only marginally helpful to schools trying to decide what to teach.

But a Johns Hopkins University study cited earlier suggests that attitudes toward work make the most difference in hiring high school graduates. Ninety-four percent of company personnel with responsibility for hiring high school graduates rated dependability as extremely important.

Another study conducted by the Wisconsin Department of Education and by the Parker Pen Company also have rated dependability as the top priority and industriousness and flexibility as significant additional factors in job success. Flexibility will become increasingly important as jobs change and people have to move to new areas.

Fostering flexibility and dependability in training for new skills will be a major goal for businesses and their employees. As a result, schools will need to concentrate on teaching those skills and attitudes. Schools of the year 2000 will be able to teach flexibility and dependability by asking students to work in teams—a major work style for the year 2000.

IMPLICATIONS

- Teacher certification requirements need to become more flexible to allow for experts outside of the educational structure to teach special classes. Educators will still review course content and evaluation procedures.
- Industry and business people will teach full- or part-time in the public schools. Schools will develop special programs to select those who will be best able to teach.
- Businesses will provide schools with equipment, personnel, and some funds—money paid for services.
- More business and professional people will take a greater interest in running for school boards and participating in other areas of school governance.
- Schools and businesses must specify their separate and mutual responsibilities in each new partnership to avoid frustration.
- Curriculum must be updated continually so schools can prepare students for newly created careers in business and industry.

- Schools will have to develop policies, programs, and facilities that will allow them to move into the area of retraining workers.
- If schools cannot immediately incorporate training programs, they will be able to use interactive cable to connect students to schools that can.
- Schools will increasingly be seen as full partners in any substantive community endeavors.
- Community coalitions will bring understanding and cohesiveness to school/business partnerships and other community efforts.
- Businesses will have to develop ways to cover for employees who are volunteering in schools, teaching or taking classes.
- Schools will need to ensure—and communities must demand—that education creates good citizens as well as good employees.
- School/business partnerships must overcome such real-world concerns as unemployment rates, the cost of equipment for education, the size of the community, and availability of business partners. The best hope is regionalizing—combining with other educational institutions, such as community colleges, and with other school districts, possibly through service agencies.

9

LONGER SCHOOL DAY
AND YEAR

THE CURRENT DEBATE

One of the major issues being debated in the eighties in most of the
education reports is extending the school day and year. The reports
contend that Japan and other countries that have longer school years
also have higher student achievement scores. Some U.S. school districts, in response to the recommendations in the reports, have added
days to the year and minutes to the day. Most school districts, however, still operate for approximately 6 hours a day and 180 days
a year.

A variety of summer-school programs are available, but many are
limited to make-up or remedial courses. Some optional programs
exist for dropouts, for students who need to work, or for students
who create discipline problems. Some day-care programs are available for additional hours to a very limited group. And, in some larger
school districts, special creative programs are available for exceptional children. Computer camps and other special programs have
begun to spring up in schools all over the United States. Despite
these signs of a growing trend, however, many of the reports on
education in the eighties reflect support for the traditional classroom
setting and day program. The idea of having a certain number of

students taught by a traditional teacher during the usual hours still prevails.

Longer school days and years could provide many educational options and alternatives for students, parents, and society. But superintendents and local school boards need to make long-range plans for the better use of their facilities and funds, their human and technological resources. Issues such as the following are under debate in the eighties as school leaders consider adding days to the year and minutes to the day:

- the quality and use of the existing instructional time,
- the time required for each student,
- the time required for each course and competency,
- the time allotted for athletics and extracurricular activities,
- the management and funding of the extended day,
- access by all students to the extended day,
- the effects on the home and society of schools remaining open longer,
- the coordination of schools with other educational, cultural, and business institutions,
- the definition of a comprehensive program, and
- the management and funding sources needed to operate a comprehensive school program on extended time.

GENERAL TRENDS

In the late 1980s, school districts throughout the United States will restructure their programs to provide longer school years. The evolution of public schooling into the nineties will include a more flexible schedule for teachers and students and an expansion of curriculum to include greater emphasis on job-training skills and lifelong learning skills, such as problem-solving, decision-making, communicating, and the use of technology to schedule programs, people, and things.

By 1990, longer school days and years will be the rule in many school systems. As this change takes effect, schools will expand their operations to include numerous activities and specific job training classes for young and adult students.

If school districts lengthen the school day to 7 hours and the school year to 210 days for all students, extended day-care will probably be a part of the schools' revised program, allowing 12% more women to enter the work force. But programs for 3- and 4-year-olds will also become common. Federal funding, business support, and direct tuition will provide day-care for both rich and poor and day-care will provide important funding support to schools.

The 21st century will bring cultural changes, too, which will be more profound than the technological changes in their effects upon us. Tomorrow's citizens and decision-makers—today's students—will be more sophisticated from exposure to the cornucopia of our technology. Their value systems will differ from those of other generations. They will have more work options, some of which don't exist today, and they will be more active in shaping their own education. They will demand schools with current technology and a variety of learning experiences. They will demand an education that prepares them to deal with new situations, problems, knowledge, and changes in the workplace. Today's kindergarten students will graduate from high school in 1998. They will reflect the changes educational leaders make today. But will school boards, administrators, and society wait too long to restructure the system?

CHANGES IN EDUCATION

Students of the 21st century will probably include toddlers, children, youth, adults, and older citizens. A typical school district may provide learning experiences and training for students ages 3 to 21 and for adults ages 21 to 80-plus. Many options could be available to students and employers. Formal schooling will be taking place in the school, the home, and other learning environments through a variety of human and technological resources. As education becomes more flexible and more relevant to society's economic needs, discipline may even cease to be a major problem. These students could have many options within the extended framework of the day and year:

- attending school 7 hours and 210 days or more, depending on their needs and ability to handle tasks;
- selecting a variety of programs, both required and elective, in academic, vocational, or enrichment programs;

- working from an interactive computer/videodisc learning station at home or school;
- working on a job and going to school;
- doing apprenticeships with master teachers;
- having opportunities for expanded time in a science laboratory, music class, art class, or vocational class; and
- having opportunities to be tutored individually or in small groups.

RUNNING THE SYSTEM

The complexities of the expanded school day will require a computer system to schedule and assign students to formal school sites or institutions. Each school district will provide creative learning environments and will plan, schedule, and operate all its programs.

Imaginative administrators will decide how to use the additional time to the best advantage, since technology will allow them to offer even more comprehensive school programs. In many cases community committees will also advise the administrators on the best use of local public schools, technical schools and community colleges, universities, public libraries, museums, and other facilities. Telecommunication systems will probably be advanced enough to knit them together, in addition to allowing many homes and schools to use data banks through systems such as the Source, Compuserve, and the Library of Congress. Many other national and international facilities will also be available to all citizens through similar means.

Community involvement under the extended school framework may expand to include cooperative arrangements among high schools, community colleges, private occupational schools, and private companies to provide education and training to adults. More funding for schools will probably result as local businesses make greater use of schools and their resources. School/business partnerships will develop according to the community committee's plan.

This plan will outline goals for combining all facilities and human resources through the latest interactive technology. A schedule for the extended day and year may involve opening all high school facilities, universities, community colleges, libraries, and museums on a 24-hour basis, 7 days a week. Such options would, of course, require adequate funding.

Apprenticeship training for businesses will be taking place in schools during the hours when most of the younger students are at home. Other social factors will affect the options available to students and parents for education and training. By 1990, if employment rises by 17% to 25%, the workweek may decline to 32 hours. As parents go home for additional hours of pleasure or work, schooling may be possible at home for 1 or 2 days a week through an interactive viewdata system for both elementary and secondary students. As school districts expand the school day and year, a trend will begin that will continue into the year 2000: Private schools may lose 10% of their enrollments to the public schools.

The expansion of the school year will have far-reaching effects on curriculum, instruction, and the instructional resources available. A core curriculum will be offered for a 9-month period, shifting electives to later in the lengthened day and year. Special tuition courses for lifelong learning will be offered in most school districts to both younger students and adults. The mobility of society will require some national, competency-based curriculum standards. The management of instruction will become easier as computers become available more to schools, classrooms, and students. In prosperous districts, computers will be available to students on a 1:4 ratio; in the poorer districts, on a 1:8 ratio. The nineties will usher in additional changes, as many school districts will operate for 210 days a year, 14 hours a day.

By the year 2000, schools in all districts may be open 7 days a week with 24-hour access to automated instruction. Direct instruction and job training for older students and adults will proceed for 16 to 18 hours a day, 210 days a year, using the school facilities at times when the younger students will be off campus. The relationships established among the private sector, the home, the community, and the school will place the public schools on a solid foundation for future survival. Time for schooling will become more important as the workweek declines to 25 hours for adults. Students and parents will have flexible schedules for work and far more leisure time to pursue the arts, self-supporting employment opportunities, and do-it-yourself projects.

THE PROMISE OF THE FUTURE

The major goals for the new learning environment will include:
- equal access to learning opportunities for all people, and to higher-level courses for minorities and women especially;
- true lifelong learning for all people;
- education of more people to higher levels of knowledge;
- less crime;
- a healthier, self-sufficient society;
- less dependence on federal funding;
- profitable and efficient schools as foreign language learning increases and technology brings other cultures to the classroom through teleconferencing or videodiscs; and
- movement toward an upper-middle-class society.

A longer school year and day will open opportunities for everyone involved: job-sharing for teachers and other educators; part-time jobs for students; job opportunities for parents; and learning experiences not available to all during the school days of the eighties. Students may, through flexible scheduling, progress at their own pace with enough time to become competent in various skills and subjects. Administrators may capitalize on the strengths and diminish the weaknesses of their staffs and may use their facilities and resources for cooperative ventures with the private sector and other educational institutions.

IMPLICATIONS

- The schools increasingly will take on a custodial role as communities take advantage of the new school schedule.
- Increased school time will make it more likely that schools will pay teachers more if communities are willing to provide funds.
- Parents may pull their children out of private schools and place them back in the public schools to take advantage of increased learning time and the longer period that schools will supervise the students.
- The capacity of schools to host community activities will increase. Programs such as adult education will flourish, but so will the cost of maintenance and operation of the school facilities.

- Schools will become even more accessible to students who wish to do enrichment or remedial work.
- School facilities will be used more cost effectively.
- The need for funds from communities and states will continue to grow.

10

LOW PUPIL-TEACHER RATIOS

INTRODUCTION

Pupil-teacher ratios may no longer be a major issue in the year 2000. Standards governing areas such as time on task, the frequency of pupil-teacher interactions in small groups of 5 or 8, and the frequency of large-group interactions, independent study, team study, computer drills, and computer applications may predominate instead. Teachers will have guidelines from learning researchers on the time needed by various students to master certain skills or bodies of knowledge. Agreements with teachers may specify the class sizes appropriate to different goals. Writing labs and discussion sections, for example, require smaller groups than classes taught by the lecture method. Thus, classes of 30 to 40 students may no longer be as common as they are today, and by traditional measures, class size will decrease.

PUPIL-TEACHER RATIO WILL DECLINE

Technological factors related to the extended school day may force dramatic changes in pupil-teacher ratios by the nineties. As elementary and secondary students work at home 1 or 2 days each week on individualized interactive programs, the ratios will fall to levels that contribute to maximum student achievement.

Teachers will teach all the students, but not every day nor all day long. Job-sharing may relieve individual teachers from having to teach large groups for long periods of the day. A masters-level biology teacher may deliver a lecture to a large group of students and then have 2 labs made up of smaller groups. Alternatively, that teacher might deliver a lecture via interactive videotape or disc through a network and not even be "at work" on that particular day.

Volunteer efforts may further reduce the pupil-teacher ratio. Retired citizens taking classes at the school and local business people may assist in supervising small groups in subject areas they know best. The former might lead discussions of civics or economics; the latter, reading or writing. Peer teaching may also become more prevalent, and in some technologies children may teach adults. There will probably be a multitude of computer users' groups to help each other through advanced networks. Children and students of all ages will have access to numerous resources through data banks. "Help with Homework" and other practical hotlines will be increasingly available to students before the turn of the 21st century.

The return to the public schools of some students previously enrolled in private schools, the entrance of adults into the school population, and new standards for the size of classes will be balanced by the availability of technology for reducing class loads and managing instruction.

CONCLUSION

Schooling will change dramatically because of factors related to new delivery systems, the extension of the school day, new funding patterns, the involvement of the private sector, and the equity issues raised in the nineties. Above all, education will address specific learning outcomes for students. As these factors come to dominate the scene, pupil-teacher ratio will recede in importance. The issue will have been resolved by the beginning of the 21st century with the implementation of computer management and instructional systems, and the fulfillment of the promise of technology for use in the classroom.

School administrators and teachers will need to look at their facilities, staff, curriculum, funds, and resources and to develop new models of learning. Some research suggests that the pupil-teacher ratio must be reduced to at least 1 teacher per 15 students before there will be significant differences in student achievement. The time has come to tailor class sizes to learning objectives, particular subjects and their levels of difficulty, ways certain subjects should be taught, learning styles of teachers and students, and other meaningful educational factors.

Marilyn Ferguson, in *The Aquarian Conspiracy*, has given educators a view of learning from the past to the present to the future in "Learning: The Emerging Paradigm." This paradigm can be a blueprint for developing new models of learning based on recent research and sound educational principles. Educational researchers are already combining the effective strategies from the past with those emerging in classrooms now using computers.

IMPLICATIONS

- Schools will make the best possible use of research and experience to guide them in allotting the right amount of time to individual students to learn various types of information or develop individual skills and talents. Thus, class sizes will vary according to students' needs and a subject's requirements.
- Schools must be able to work with groups of students with varying interests and abilities. Students may be a part of several groups during the school day.
- Teachers' strengths will be a consideration in their class assignments. Teachers who are good at large-group work may be assigned to lecture; those who excel at small-group work may be assigned to one-on-one instruction; those who communicate well on television may be assigned to teach in that way.
- Teamwork among school staff will help to keep assignments enjoyable and varied.
- Administrators will require an even higher level of management skills to deal with outcome-oriented education and the expanded role of the schools.

11

CURRICULUM AND STUDENT STANDARDS

By the year 2000—and probably much sooner—students will not only be able to receive a thorough grounding in the fundamentals, but will also be able to select from a greatly expanded range of additional curriculum offerings. The following discussion of future curriculum standards explores trends that will be of major impact. It is not intended to touch on all the areas school planners are concerned with today, but should provide material for fruitful community-wide discussion.

Today, a school district's curriculum offerings are frequently limited by two major constraints. First, districts can offer only those courses that their current staff are equipped to teach. Second, schools can usually offer only those courses that interest enough students to justify the expenditure of funds and teachers' time. In the future, neither of these will necessarily limit the curriculum range. Computers and electronic communication will bring teaching resources from miles away to the small school. Students from many communities will be able to enroll in specialized subjects normally commanding small enrollments.

By the year 1990, with the extension of the school day and year, 75% of school districts will offer a core, 9-month program in skills that are considered basic areas in the curriculum. About 95% of all high schools will require a basic-skills competency test by the year 2000, compared with about 65% by the year 1990.

The concept of the basic core-course structure will be expanded. The liberal arts will be an important part of these basics, particularly writing and other forms of communication. The writing curriculum, however, will draw on the latest research and will build on the success of models such as the Bay Area Writing Project. The emphasis of most writing instruction will not be on the mechanics of language and composition—although these will be integrated throughout the process of writing. Instead, the emphasis of most writing instruction will be on writing, *rewriting*, and learning by doing.

Computers will be an integral part of this teaching process. Word processing, which allows students to rewrite almost effortlessly, will become commonplace. In fact, students will probably learn word processing as another basic skill.

This type of teaching will begin in the very early grades. In fact, some school districts are already experimenting with this approach. Researcher John Henry Martin, working with IBM, has followed kindergarten students who were taught to use computers as a way to learn both reading and writing. The results were startling. According to a 1984 Educational Testing Service evaluation, on standardized reading tests, kindergarten and first-grade students in these programs progressed faster than national-norm students, an average of 15 percentile points. The progress was steady, lasting throughout the one-year evaluation period. Males made as much gain as females, blacks as much gain as whites, high socioeconomic as low socioeconomic, and finally, students with high initial ability progressed on an even basis with those of low initial ability. The all-too-familiar pattern of certain groups falling behind from their first days in school did not occur. Individuals, of course, did not all attain the same high scores. But individuals scoring lower were not likely to be a part of one group, racial, economic, or otherwise.

Writing and speaking will be emphasized in all subjects. Because many drill and practice exercises will probably be left to interactive machines, teachers will be able to concentrate on teaching more sophisticated communication skills during their class sessions. Students will also be taught higher levels of mathematics and simple computer programming and authoring languages. Other basics will include the arts, social studies, scientific inquiry, and physical and mental fitness. Preparing students to be more active citizens and to get along with other people will also be among the basics.

During the remainder of the time before graduation, students will select courses from a variety of special-interest, enrichment, and advanced-level courses. Those who attain minimum competency in the basic skills of reading, writing, speaking, listening, viewing, analyzing, mathematical reasoning, and scientific inquiry will be able to select their own courses or units to develop higher levels of reasoning and thinking. This process will be aided by the expansion of technology in computer-managed curriculum design.

DESIGNING THE NEW CURRICULUM

Curriculum specialists will spend the next 10 years developing comprehensive design-and-delivery systems for the most sophisticated program of studies ever offered to American students. Various models will be available for the consideration of local school districts, including banks of courses, competencies, learning units, and item banks for testing and evaluation.

These models, competencies, and test items will be based on a growing knowledge of what is needed to function outside of school. What skills, interests, curiosities, and plans do students pursue in kindergarten, first, seventh, and tenth grades? What general knowledge is needed by a college student, by an entry-level job applicant? Of course, much of this is flexible and will change. But scientists who study learning will be able to set reasonable expectations based on studies of child development and teachers will be able to establish appropriate learning outcomes for individual students. With knowledge of real-world requirements, curriculum planners will be able to set guidelines for the skills needed for early elementary, late elementary, junior high, and secondary-level students.

Realistic expectations represent only one problem that will be easier for future course planners to handle. A second problem, managing students who may race ahead or fall behind their age-level peers, will also be easier to deal with. Teacher assignments will be more flexible when much of the study can be managed independently by the student with the aid of the computer. Artificial divisions dictated by textbook length will give way to teacher–authored/modified computer software. Students will not talk about the grade they are in; they will talk about the outcome topic, issue, job experience, project, or community application with which they are working. All the time, however, students, teachers, and parents will have the knowledge and understanding of essential skills needed to pursue student goals in the world outside the school.

Learning modules will be available to infants, young children, youth, and various adult groups, including older citizens. All learning activities on school campuses, in art and nature museums, in public libraries, and in other formal and informal learning environments will be identified as part of the curriculum and will be assigned to particular courses.

The curriculum will be published and communicated to all citizens who live in each local school district. It will be kept up to date through a computer-managed competency bank that will identify learning objectives for students and ways to evaluate the objectives, comparing them with individual student performance. This management system will provide administrators with a tool to individualize the curriculum for every student and lead toward development of a daily plan for each student. Parents and guardians will be able to monitor their children's achievements better because, in many cases, the day's assignments will be based on mastering specific competencies. Teachers will draw on the computer-managed system to match the best possible teaching techniques with the needs of each student.

STANDARDS

By the year 2000, students will compete more with themselves, less with each other in their daily work. And they will be consistently monitored to ensure that they achieve the highest levels of competence for their individual abilities and talents.

Individual education plans, today usually a part of the program for exceptional children only, will be possible for every student. And all students, regardless of their problems or expectations, will have the opportunity to achieve their goals with fewer time constraints, fewer comparisons to other students, and fewer limitations in ways to learn.

Young students, adults, and older citizens might all be learning together in some classes, labs, libraries, and work stations. Gifted and talented students in particular will be able to take advantage of advanced university courses, sometimes taught half a continent away, while maintaining relationships with their fellow students in the public schools.

These individualized standards, however, may only be developed at some cost. During the short term, schools face severe concerns about increases in the dropout rate. The experience in most states that have instituted across-the-board standards or competency requirements has been that marginal students are more likely to drop out. Until a more flexible system of individualized standards is developed, this trend will continue. Those who impose "quick-fix" standards must beware of the consequences for many students.

All students will be expected to master a core of competencies, reach learning outcomes for a certain level of literacy that is still to be defined. Choices about those core competencies that will be offered to all students will have to be made between now and 1990 to ensure their preparation for success in the lifelong learning process.

INCREASING RESPONSIBILITIES

The high schools in many school districts in the year 2000 may be providing 80% of the training necessary for entering the job market, as opposed to about 25% in 1990. In addition, school districts and community colleges will, by then, provide 80% of undergraduate preparation. By the turn of the 21st century, school districts will be among the primary sources of career preparation for their students and 40% of all high schools and community colleges in the United States will be the delivery systems for career preparation. Many courses for adult learners will include a tuition fee. Based on community education courses now being offered, we predict that in 1990 only 50% of the nation's schools will be offering special tuition courses, but by 2000, 80% will.

TECHNOLOGY AND THE CURRICULUM

The advancement of the technologies and the networking capabilities within school districts will provide students access to all the new basics and even greater learning opportunities in the following: 1) advanced-level sciences, including physics, chemistry, anatomy, and biogenetics; 2) advanced-level mathematics, including calculus and statistics; 3) foreign languages, including conversational skills, reading, and writing skills; 4) communications, including reading of the classics, debate, discussion and rhetoric, technical writing, problem-solving, thinking skills, authoring software for computers and videodisc interactive technologies, and the production of video films and discs and digital audio discs; 5) international studies—cultural, economic, and political; 6) arts education—visual arts, drama, dance, music, commercial art, electronic arts, and folk art; 7) technical and applied sciences for career training, such as data processing, telecommunications, robotics, public health, geriatrics, and laser technology; 8) studies in citizenship and law, including political systems, paralegal work, consumer information, and mass media education; 9) human relations and philosophy; 10) futures studies, such as forecasting, decision-making, and conservation; 11) home survival, including do-it-yourself projects, problem-solving management, and technology literacy.

Even today a college education may ultimately result in a student earning less income than a graduate of a technical and applied training program. That situation may affect the percentage of the youth population that will attend traditional universities or colleges. Three-fourths of the youth population will enter training programs based on society's changing job market, whether they pursue a college degree or not. Cetron, in his book *Jobs of the Future*, provides a blueprint for future career opportunities for youth and adult. He indicates the jobs that will emerge often 1990. (See chart on page 122.)

GIFTED AND TALENTED STUDENTS

As the year 2000 approaches, the category of "gifted and talented" students may include an increasing number with talents, not just those with intelligence measured by tests emphasizing vocabulary. The new definitions, moreover, will measure the students' innate potential as well as their present levels of achievement.

Psychologist Dr. Perry Buffington of Atlanta, Georgia, says the idea that creativity is always linked to intelligence is a myth. He believes that high intelligence does not guarantee creativity. Only moderate intelligence is needed to excel creatively, especially in art and music, according to Buffington. In IQs above 120, intelligence seems to have little relationship to creativity. Buffington has identified five stages of creative thought: 1) orientation—to define a problem and identify its dimensions; 2) overpreparation—to flood oneself with information related to the problem; 3) incubation—to forget the problem for a while, to let it simmer; 4) illumination—the "aha experience"; and 5) verification—the testing period. He says that creativity is a combination of intuitiveness, enthusiasm, flexibility, independence, initiative, and intelligence. The implications of Buffington's theories for education today are worth noting, for these are the same characteristics desired of the ideal worker by most employers. Buffington has not only described the stages of the creative process, but has closely described the way most people learn.

By 1990, as even more rigid standards begin to be enforced, there may be less creativity and flexibility in the learning process. As programs for the gifted and talented expand, the average student will continue in programs requiring more routine, rote-learning tasks. Schools must do everything possible to ensure that students are not locked out by rigid standards and prevented from reaching their individual potential. A potential diplomat, for example, should not be limited in pursuing higher education due to a deficiency in geometry.

The curriculum in the year 2000 will allow the gifted and talented to move at exceptional rates through independent study programs. These and other students will be provided many options as they master their basic core competencies. They will be allowed to move into the university setting, to attend events and lectures held on college campuses, or to receive from anywhere in the world, via interactive TV, an on-the-spot event for researching or reporting. Electronic access to advanced levels of courses in science, mathematics, literature, the humanities, languages, and other subjects will become more commonplace. Many students of the high school graduating class of the year 2000 may be enrolled in college at the same time. The key to advanced levels of study in the year 2000 will be the variety of options provided through networked systems of higher education and easy access to hands-on experiences in the many learning laboratories and futuristic schools.

IMPLICATIONS

New curricula and standards will affect society in many ways.
- Students will be better prepared to work and make the complex decisions that will be necessary in the 21st century.
- Business communities will benefit from a more highly educated and better-trained work force.
- The new standards will address the equity concerns stemming from the old absolute and unbending standards of the past.
- Greater involvement of school staff and community will be required in developing standards to assure that staff members understand their roles in pursuing them and the community understands its role in providing resources to achieve them.
- State legislators and governors will need to become better informed about education so they can help, not harm schools in their rush to set standards. They must also be committed to providing financial support for schools to make it possible for them to meet the standards. If legislators and governors play an increased role in setting standards, then they will be held increasingly accountable for decisions and their enforcement in this area.
- State legislators, governors, and local school administrators and school boards increasingly will work together in the best interests of schools and the students they serve.

12

TEACHING AND PROFESSIONAL STANDARDS

THE CURRENT DEBATE

Teachers are often criticized for being unable to teach. National reports cite low test performance among teachers, low salaries, a lack of respect for the profession and a variety of other problems, such as student discipline and drug abuse, for the decline in the quality of teaching. Plans for merit pay, career ladders, performance appraisal, and new tests for measuring teacher competence are being debated and implemented in some states. Polls show support for pay based on performance. However, merit plans and career ladders must include a provision to address the issue of parity or equity with the professions. Performance-appraisal or evaluation instruments and quality-assurance programs to measure teachers' and administrators' accountability are being developed.

THE PROBLEMS OF THE PROFESSION

Teacher education programs are under scrutiny for accepting students who have less academic talent than a decade ago and who place in the lower ranks of their high school graduating classes. A Rand report released in August 1984, entitled *The Coming Crisis in Teaching*, indicated that the nation's teaching force will soon suffer serious shortages unless the profession is restructured. The report analyzed recruitment and retention patterns, the quality of teachers, and the attractiveness of the profession. It suggests evidence that:

- New recruits to the profession are less qualified academically than those who are leaving through retirement or finding higher-paying jobs;
- The number of new entrants is insufficient to meet the coming demand;
- Talented women and minorities have greater career options outside of teaching and therefore are not as likely to be attracted to teaching as they were formerly;
- Most academically-able recruits leave the profession within a very short time; and
- Shortages of qualified teachers in science and mathematics will grow over the next few years into a more generalized shortage.

Causes cited in the Rand report for these problems are: low salaries, poor working conditions, lack of sufficient teacher preparation, lack of professionalism, and lack of administrative support. Unless major changes occur, the report suggests that the least academically qualified teachers in history could become the tenured teaching force for the next 2 generations of American schoolchildren.

Teacher pay rose an estimated 6.3% from 1983 to 1984—from $20,715 to an estimated $22,019. Below is a state-by-state breakdown.

	Rank	*Quartile* (see key)	
U.S. average			**$22,019**
Alabama	42	L	18,000
Alaska	1	U	36,564
Arizona	22	M	21,605
Arkansas	49	L	16,929
California	5	U	26,403
Colorado	16	M	22,895
Connecticut	19	M	22,624
Delaware	24	M	20,925
District of Columbia	3	U	27,659
Florida	34	M	19,545

	Rank	Quartile (see key)	
Georgia	39	L	18,505
Hawaii	10	U	24,357
Idaho	38	M	18,640
Illinois	12	U	23,345
Indiana	22	M	21,587
Iowa	29	M	20,140
Kansas	33	M	19,598
Kentucky	32	M	19,780
Louisiana	36	M	19,100
Maine	48	L	17,328
Maryland	11	U	24,095
Massachusetts	20	M	22,500
Michigan	2	U	28,877
Minnesota	9	U	24,480
Mississippi	51	L	15,895
Missouri	35	M	19,300
Montana	26	M	20,657
Nebraska	37	M	18,785
Nevada	13	U	23,000
New Hampshire	47	L	17,376
New Jersey	14	M	23,044
New Mexico	25	M	20,760
New York	4	U	26,750
North Carolina	41	L	18,014
North Dakota	27	M	20,363
Ohio	23	M	21,421
Oklahoma	40	L	18,490
Oregon	17	M	22,833
Pennsylvania	18	M	22,800
Rhode Island	7	U	24,641
South Carolina	45	L	17,500
South Dakota	50	L	16,480
Tennessee	44	L	17,900
Texas	30	M	20,100
Utah	28	M	20,256

	Rank	Quartile (*see key*)	
Vermont	43	L	17,931
Virginia	31	M	19,867
Washington	6	U	24,780
West Virginia	46	L	17,482
Wisconsin	14	M	23,000
Wyoming	8	U	24,500

Source: NEA Research

U = Upper quartile
M = Middle quartiles
L = Lower quartile

The average SAT scores of high school students intending to major in education today are 812; that compares with 987 for engineering students and 893 for all students who took the test. (The majority of classroom teachers entering the profession in the United States in 1984 were women with relatively low SAT scores.) The need to raise SAT scores for admission to schools of education will be debated and many schools will be considering what the standard will be. Some recommendations include raising requisite SAT scores for entering teachers to levels comparable with other professions, such as law, medicine, and engineering, and requiring a 3.2 grade point average for entering the professional level of teacher training.

INNOVATIVE PAY PROGRAMS

Today, according to David Imig of the American Association of Colleges for Teacher Education, "teacher education is and ought to be the next focus of those trying to improve the schools." Many new career-ladder and merit-pay programs are being instituted across the country. Among the career-ladder plans, the Charlotte-Mecklenberg System of Charlotte, North Carolina, is being hailed as a comprehensive plan, with support from the North Carolina legislature, which exempted the school system from the Teacher Tenure Law. Tennessee and Florida are also implementing new merit-pay programs. New, tougher teacher competency standards and testing programs are being established in teacher training colleges and universities.

In school districts where merit-pay plans have been considered or implemented, there have been some problems. School districts—including those whose salaries are $4,000 or more below the national average—must guard against career-ladder and merit plans having adverse effects on the regular pay raises of all teachers, allowing only those who acquire status on the ladder to receive pay increases. Other factors relating to merit plans need careful attention. Will the management of the plans be people-intensive? How much paperwork will be added to the regular responsibilities of teachers and administrators? How will schools deal with pressure from parents to have their children in career status teachers' classes? We predict that many school districts will need to raise all teachers' salaries as part of initiating merit-pay plans: The parity or equity issue must be faced nationally before teacher standards can be improved.

The average starting wage for teachers in 1984 was $14,500—$5,000 lower than positions in sales or business administration and more than $12,000 below entry-level jobs in engineering and computer science. The teaching profession cannot hope to attract the most qualified graduates until this disparity is addressed.

In fact, over the past decade, salaries from private industry have often increased by as much as 95%, while teacher salaries have increased by only 76%. The following chart, based on U.S. Department of Labor information, shows the comparison:

1974	Profession	1984
$ 8,223	Teacher	$14,500
8,685	Laboratory Technician	17,761
8,892	Librarian	19,344
9,672	Economist	20,484
11,040	Accountant	20,176
10,088	Sanitation Worker	20,280
10,176	Statistician	22,416
11,284	Radio Broadcaster	20,800
11,925	Bus Driver (Metro)	22,906
11,546	Computer Analyst	24,864

1974	*Profession*	*1984*
11,556	Engineer	26,844
13,485	Construction Worker	23,126
14,820	Plumber	24,180
16,801	Social Worker	23,907
18,666	Purchasing Director	37,374
19,634	Personnel Director	42,978

By 1990 the teacher profile may change as a result of the performance-based merit pay and career advancement incentives starting to be offered across the United States today. The federal government will provide direction for these programs, but funding will come through state and local sources. Federal grants, such as Chapter 2 of the Educational Improvement and Consolidation Act and the Job Training Partnership Act, will be used primarily for a one-time boost.

EDUCATION AND TRAINING PROGRAMS

In 1990 teacher education programs may expand to 5 years to allow more training in the disciplines, in human growth and development, and in educational psychology and learning theory. Upgraded programs are already being planned in 19% of the nation's teacher education programs. The University of New Hampshire, for example, has instituted a 5-year education program that incorporates both practical classroom experience and additional time for academic study.

Teacher education programs will offer courses to emphasize new core competencies and to meet the higher teacher standards. The new general competencies will stress not only knowledge of given subject areas, but greater knowledge of the learning processes that cut across subject areas—thinking/reasoning skills, communication, and technology. All teachers graduating and receiving teacher certification by 1990 will have to be able to use the new technologies in the classroom and have to demonstrate a certain standard of literacy in that area. Literacy by this definition will include the following abilities:

- how to design instruction for a computer format;
- how to develop questions or techniques for teaching students to use computers and interactive videodiscs;

- how to select courseware and software; and
- how to design individual learning techniques using multisystems of print and nonprint technologies. Literacy programs for teachers may also include instructional management systems and effective teaching techniques.

Training programs for beginning teachers, however, may be difficult to implement because of funding problems and traditions. Retraining of all teachers currently in local school districts will also be a challenge, since funding for retraining may still be minimal. If funding is scarce in certain districts, we predict that incentives for teachers and other educators to purchase their own learning equipment will be considered by various hardware companies. Educators will need to have access at home to computer technology—and to the many training opportunities available through computer or video networks—in order to use it in the classroom.

We predict that higher standards will prevail at all levels of teaching. Education students will be required to master a battery of skills prior to entering the profession. Additionally, beginning teachers will work as interns and will have to demonstrate proficiency and pass substantive knowledge examinations before attaining career status. With higher standards of teacher performance, businesses will try to attract teachers into the private sector. The issue of teacher tenure will not be as important to teachers who are able to get jobs in a broader market.

Schools will have a broader range of personnel from which to draw for staffing. The resources of older teachers will be used on a part-time basis through job-sharing. With shorter workweeks being a norm, senior citizens and other volunteers may contribute more hours to the schools than they can now; however, volunteer association leaders caution that schools will need to monitor these activities through actual contracts with some volunteers. Volunteer burnout may become a real problem.

The ability to program higher levels of artificial intelligence into teaching machines will provide the human teacher with powerful tools to assist in teaching higher levels of thinking and learning. With advances in understanding human learning and brain research, teachers will be able to design instruction to meet the individual learner's needs and goals for academic achievement.

We predict that by the year 2000, school districts will have greater pride in their teachers. Excellence will be seen as the key to teaching in the 21st century. Teaching will have become a science as well as an art, and teachers will be well trained not only in their subject areas, but in the understanding of mental and physical growth and development, thinking processes, curriculum and instruction design and implementation, educational psychology, technology-assisted instruction and management, learning styles theory, and the development and evaluation of teaching materials.

The teacher of the 20th century who stood in front of 35 or more students and delivered information to them for recitation, memorization, and test-taking will change to a 21st-century resource teacher who will guide students through learning experiences by designing appropriate modifications in the curriculum.

Teachers in the year 2000 will implement special plans for individual students and will serve as mentors or tutors by following them through a process for attaining skills, concepts, and a higher level of reasoning. A variety of learning-resource teachers, area specialists, master teachers, guidance counselors, physical and mental health specialists, volunteers, and peers will work together to design, implement, and coach all students on the road toward the desired goals, expectations, and excellence in academic achievement and career preparation demanded by the complex society.

We predict that teachers in the 21st century will be teaching by choice in one of the most respected professions of the day. Salaries and working conditions will have improved for all teachers from the dark days of the past. Performance-based merit pay will be in effect in most school districts. Paid sabbaticals will be offered to professional educators in many school districts; often districts themselves will pay for teacher retraining—this will probably occur 3 or 4 times during teachers' professional careers.

Professional teachers' associations will demand accountability of their own members, considering it vital to maintaining respect for their profession. Superior teachers will be rewarded for teaching and supervising in the most difficult learning processes. They will be the instructional designers. Other teachers will be given assignments appropriate to their abilities. Many will be able to perform in the management of data and materials related to teaching.

Teacher education programs will be expanded to 5 and 6 years or longer by the year 2000, depending on the area of teaching. Standards for students entering programs will be strengthened to include tests of speaking, reading, and writing, achievement in a liberal arts program, and performance in an interview process. All teacher education programs will define competencies that will include the latest findings in the research on human learning.

Upon entering school districts, teachers will be placed in training programs based on their individual needs as appraised during their internships. Investments in staff development programs for teachers will be necessary to ensure the quality of student achievement and the maintenance of student standards.

We think that school districts by the 21st century will learn that rapid changes in telecommunications and technology will demand a constant reevaluation of programs, personnel, and funds. The changes will affect organizations of schools and staffing patterns. Up to 25% of administrative functions may shift to instructional support. This will create more jobs for teachers and learning resource personnel at a time when options for job-sharing and flexible working hours will be more readily available.

The teaching profession will offer many incentives to its prospective members: programs to bring teachers' skills up to date and to permit them to study at universities while being paid, opportunities for them to choose the time of the year and time of the day in which to work, and opportunities to select activities and techniques best suited to their abilities. As the workweek becomes shorter for most Americans, teachers will also benefit. They will be able to choose whether they wish to work 25 hours a week or as many as 50 hours a week, if they prefer to do so.

Teachers' unions may be less contentious in the nineties or in the 21st century. As teaching and pay conditions improve, union membership may decline, as it will in other unions. Even if teacher union membership remains high, unions will be operating in an atmosphere of lower public support for unions. Thus, we expect teacher unions to take on the character of the American Bar Association or the American Medical Association, rather than the "skilled trade" direction they have taken since the late 1960s.

We predict that changes in society, methodologies, and technology will require basic changes in the roles of teachers. Differentiation of teaching roles will become a must in the management of classrooms and home learning. Instructional teams will be established with members accepting various roles in educating students. The management of instruction will require well-trained teachers. Salaries will match the competencies and tasks of the individual team members. Teacher education programs will change dramatically; some teachers will be trained in schools of education, some in business schools, some in technical schools, and some in law and medical schools. Teaching will emerge as a highly respected, well-paid profession in the 21st century.

IMPLICATIONS

- Teacher unions will play a key role in how rapidly changes occur in professional standards.
- Teacher unions will recognize that if they resist professional standards too strongly, their influence will diminish. They will move instead toward instituting accountability measures themselves through such measures as peer review boards, a model used in the medical and legal professions today.
- Communities must be willing to provide the dollars needed to provide equitable compensation for teachers. Teachers' salaries will have to be at least commensurate with the pay scale of others whose positions require at least a bachelors degree.
- Working conditions for teachers will have to be improved if the schools are to maintain quality teaching staffs and avoid teacher shortages.
- The status of teachers, administrators, and other educational groups must be improved if schools are to be in a position to attract the best.
- Merit- or incentive-pay programs must be considered and tied to performance. Schools will need to deal with the issue of teacher competency testing and any test must measure specific criteria that bear on teacher success in educating students.
- Schools must develop sound recruitment programs to attract high-quality employees and help them maintain their professional status through effective in-service, continuing-education programs.

- Schools may want to try to attract back some of the people who have been lost to business and industry.
- Teachers must be willing and adept at incorporating new teaching technologies.
- Teachers, administrators, and other school staff members must become even more adept at communicating internally and externally.
- When the school year is lengthened, some teachers may wish to work longer days. Communities can enhance their school revenue base by planning ways those teachers' services can be marketed to the private sector.
- Those from business and industry who are recruited to teach in the schools must be used effectively; standards of performance must be developed for their contributions.
- Teacher certification will become an issue as more people from outside the teaching profession enter it to share their specific knowledge, skills, or talents.

EPILOGUE

In Gaston County, North Carolina, recently a questionnaire was sent out by a community-based planning group, which included school administrators, to determine whether the community was willing to raise taxes to support public schools. The community is poor; 42% of its households are headed by single women. Ninety percent of the questionnaires were returned. Overwhelmingly they responded, "I would be willing to pay more money if it would mean that my children would receive more math, reading, science, and computer opportunities."

In Omaha, Nebraska, at a major conference attended by the state governor, their U.S. senators, and several hundred business people and concerned citizens, a woman stood up in the audience and asked, "What am I going to do? I am only going to get $2 a bushel for corn this year. I cannot afford to pay any more for schools." The response was, "If someone told you that there was a new wonder drug on the market that would save your children from suffering the debilitation of operating at 75% of their mental capacity through their working lives, would you buy it?" She said, "Yes, of course."

If improved teachers and schools are the medicine needed to bring the United States back to its full potential, we will have to find the funds, the means, and the ways.

Jobs of the Future

OCCUPATION	NUMBER OF WORKERS REQUIRED BY 1990	ENTRY SALARY	MID-CAREER SALARY	YEARS OF COLLEGE REQUIRED
Housing Rehabilitation Technicians	1,750,000	$14,000	$24,000	0
Energy Conservation Technicians	1,500,000	13,000	26,000	0
Hazardous Waste Disposal Technicians	1,500,000	15,000	28,000	2
Industrial Laser Process Technicians	600,000	30,000	50,000	0
Robotic Engineers	500,000	23,000	35,000	4
Geriatric Social Workers	450,000	15,000	21,000	4
Materials Utilization Technicians	400,000	15,000	24,000	4
Holographic Inspectors	200,000	18,000	20,000	2
Home Electronic Interactive Systems Technicians	200,000	15,000	21,000	0
Microcomputer Diagnosticians	200,000	20,000	35,000	2
Energy Auditors	150,000	12,000	16,000	0
Genetic Engineers	150,000	23,000	38,000	Grad School
Telemarketing Advertising & Scenario Writers	110,000	18,000	35,000	4
Telemarketing Specialists—recording/ customer order take-off	80,000	15,000	30,000	0
Telemarketing Sales Program Supervisors	65,000	25,000	100,000	4
Teletext Computer Specialists— composition, format, editing	65,000	16,000	40,000	4
Telemarketing Computer Programmers	60,000	20,000	35,000	0
Telemarketing Audio-Visual Technicians	50,000	25,000	40,000	4
Telemarketing Sales—shipping/billing clerks/supers	50,000	8,000	18,000	0
Teletext Broadcast Communications Engineers	40,000	20,000	40,000	4
Teletext Interactive Correspondent	30,000	18,000	25,000	4
Teletext Specialists—marketing	30,000	18,000	40,000	4
Teletext Specialists—software programming	30,000	18,000	30,000	0
Teletext Specialists—CATV liaison & scheduling	30,000	17,000	38,000	0
Battery Technicians—fuel cells	25,000	9,000	14,000	0
Computer Axial Tomography Technologists	25,000	12,000	20,000	2
Positron Emission Technologists	25,000	12,000	20,000	4
Teletext Operations Supervisors	25,000	20,000	34,000	0
Teletext Senior Editors & Directors	25,000	30,000	50,000	4
Teletext Supervisors—library, research, copy, distribution	20,000	20,000	30,000	4

Excerpted from *Jobs of the Future*, by Marvin Cetron with Marcia Appel. Copyright © 1984 by Marvin Cetron and Marcia Appel. Reprinted by permission of McGraw-Hill Book Company.

APPENDIX A:

FUTURE CONDITIONS— IMPLICATIONS FOR SCHOOL PLANNERS

This section will review the major points of the preceding chapters. It is a synthesis to be used by long-range planners and forecasters of the school system.

Since this book is forecasting events 15 years from now, it is essential to review not only what is familiar in the school environment, but also what could cause it to change. Certain outside factors that play a small part in 1985 may have a major impact in the year 2000. Such technological changes as computers, telecommunication, and videodiscs comprise one such area. Business needs for training form another. Lifestyle changes for the family form another.

The national education reform reports of the 1980s made recommendations based on priorities connected with college entrance. The 70% of our youth who may not even enroll in college and the adults who may require retraining every 5 or 10 years were not considered. Also, the recommendations did not deal sufficiently with the changes in technology, our business world, and the prospective work force. Schools should seriously consider the recommendations in the reports, but they should also consider what is missing. Here are a few items that should have been covered in more depth.

FUTURE HOMEWORK—WILL IT BE DONE AT HOME?

Some reports recommend that students be given more homework. The reports deplore the decrease in homework assignments. In the future, however, the purposes of homework may be achieved in a different way. Drill and practice may be handled on the computer during the school day—at home or at school. What's more, a computer program will correct the homework immediately and recommend a conference with the teacher or a different assignment for further practice. Self-discipline will be encouraged through independent study or group study. Students will have to discipline themselves to be able to contribute, punctually, to the overall efforts of their study teams.

FUTURE TEACHER PREPARATION— WHAT EFFECT WILL IT HAVE?

The reports recommend higher standards for preparation of new teachers. But if present trends continue, the overall demand for new teachers will not reach 5% of the current number of teachers before 1990. If universities concentrate only on better preparation for new teachers, the nation's overall teaching staff will still need considerable updating. Thus, the new standards could have little immediate effect. The reports also recommend that teachers already practicing be given inservice training and even sabbaticals. But will there be money under present funding systems to support this extra training? Will newly trained teachers reenter the same schools they left, where some subjects may be taught the same old way and where students continue to be grouped according to standardized tests?

FUTURE EDUCATIONAL STANDARDS—WHO WILL HAVE THE OPPORTUNITY?

The national reports recommend greater access for minority students and for girls to quality education, including math, science, and computer courses. At the same time, the standards for entrance into these classes are supposed to be raised. But will more students be able to enroll in these classes if standards for entrance are raised? Will the technology of the future ensure that the students are well enough prepared for advanced classes? Will we have enough money to make sure that needed technology is available to all students—not just the brightest and the richest?

Since the national reform reports have been issued, 40 states have taken action. Several, both rich and poor, have passed sales taxes to go to schools, increased teachers' salaries, added science and mathematics programs, and purchased computers. But in the richer communities, parents have donated additional computers to the schools, sent their children to computer camps, and enhanced computer programs in the schools by providing PTA monies to buy software.

Less wealthy communities may raise teacher salaries but may not be able to provide monies for them to learn new skills. They can require new science courses, but may not be able to update the laboratories where the science classes are held. They can reinstitute English requirements for all 4 years of high school, but parents cannot buy word processing packages to give students practice at home in writing English compositions.

Businesses, the federal government, the state governments, and the agencies of higher education must see the necessity of coordinating planning to ensure even distribution of equipment, training, and evaluation resources. Without coordination, we could aggravate our problems rather than solve them. The progress we have made in providing for equal opportunity is at stake.

FUTURE CONDITIONS—WHO WILL ACT?

Finally, the national reform reports tell us that if our schools were better, our labor force would be better. Are they right? If we institute longer school days, longer school years, more stringent requirements, and better teacher preparation, will we produce a competitive work force, a healthy economy?

The national reform reports provide suggestions on what should be done to improve our schools. This book has told us how schools must work with business if we are to have a labor force skilled in tomorrow's jobs. But neither reports nor books can act. The answer to whether schools can prepare students for tomorrow's economy depends on who acts and on what they do.

The future could be bleak. We could find that the only people who will be able to both take action and continue what they have started are those in privileged communities. We must recognize that technology is accelerating social and economic, as well as scientific, changes in our society. If we allow technology to grow at will, it will flourish in those environments that can purchase it and plan for it. Technology will leave behind those who have been left behind before—at a faster pace. No one will win. At some point, those left behind will place the burden of their unproductivity on the shoulders of the entire economy.

In the crises of this century, we have allowed schools to be acted upon rather than to be one of the main actors. It is in the hands of our communities and our schools to answer the question of whether we will shape our own social and economic future or allow technology to lead us to new crises in 1990, 1995, and 2000.

The purpose of this appendix is to outline the important future conditions which planners should keep in mind when they are developing plans for action in their own communities. Since so much national attention has been directed toward the national education reform reports, their recommendations are used as a framework for discussion.

Before planners review these recommendations in the light of future conditions, however, they must recognize the two major limitations of the reports.

These issues must be considered in addressing recommendations found in national education reform reports:

1. The reports discuss how to produce a better college student, but say little about how to produce a more productive worker.
2. The reports discuss youth, but give little attention to adults. Adults will need to be reeducated and retrained every 5 to 10 years to meet the technological demands of the workplace. Public schools will be an important base for this learning.

REPORT RECOMMENDATIONS

A useful way to conceptualize the hundreds of comments in the major national reports produced by commissions, task forces, and individuals is to ask 4 questions:

1. How well do we expect our schools to perform?
   (STANDARDS, EXPECTATIONS, REQUIREMENTS FOR STUDENTS)
2. What is the content of the school year and how is it arranged?
   (CURRICULUM GOALS AND INSTRUCTIONAL DELIVERY)
3. How good are the people carrying out the program?
   (STAFF QUALITY AND RESPONSIBILITIES)
4. How should the planners and decision-makers help?
   (ADMINISTRATIVE, FEDERAL, STATE, AND LOCAL RESPONSIBILITIES)

The report recommendations do not answer some questions. These answers must be developed in each school system. A framework for dealing with the reports' recommendations can be found in *Excellence in Our Schools . . . Making It Happen*, published by the American Association of School Administrators. Our concern is that a major portion of the reports deal with secondary schools and requirements for admission to college. Little attention is given to the elementary schools or students who may not choose to attend college.

In the following sections, we will review the principal recommendations of these national task forces and comment on how elements of the future environment may shape how the recommendations should be considered. These comments may assist school systems as they develop improvement plans and address the recommendations.

RECOMMENDATIONS: STANDARDS, EXPECTATIONS, REQUIREMENTS

The reports propose higher performance from the schools in the following ways:

1. More rigorous and measurable standards;
2. Greater expectations of academic performance and student conduct;
3. More rigorous college admission requirements;
4. Upgraded textbooks;

5. More homework;
6. Class attendance and behavior codes that are enforced;
7. More intense and productive academic experience.

Two of the reports focus on the circumstances surrounding teaching:

1. The organization of subjects—how their structure enhances or detracts from achievement;
2. The introduction of skills;
3. The distribution of resources for learning and their placement to maximize achievement;
4. The satisfaction of both parents and members of the community without school-age children;
5. The hidden curriculum—when problem-solving skills are introduced, when fact-finding is required;
6. Recognition of what we don't know about learning;
7. Our organization for finding answers to what we don't know.

The reports recognize that secondary schools lack a focus on leadership and goals. A Carnegie Foundation report states:

With society requiring that schools take on the role of parents, health agencies, ethical and moral leaders, providers of arts appreciation and skills, and redressers of the ills of the disadvantaged and disabled, resources are scattered and so is school leadership.

The reports want quality assurance. Many of them use words such as:

More frequent testing with standardized tests; teacher and administrator hiring on the basis of performance; teacher and administrator promotion on the basis of performance; tests that are linked to the curriculum.

THE NEED FOR INFORMATION

Teachers and administrators will cringe at the notion that what underlies many of these recommendations is the need for more information gathered more frequently within the classroom, within the individual school building, across the school district, and across the state.

The fact is inescapable, however. The public needs to know whether the curriculum is organized effectively. We need to be able to observe teacher and administrator performance frequently so that we will have the evidence we need to support our conclusions concerning quality. We need to have systematic surveys of community opinions and needs and to know what tasks other agencies can perform better than the schools. And we need to see whether conditions change.

Report authors recommend that administrative burdens be removed from teachers, but their proposed standards will result in just the opposite. Even if schools have enough money to hire additional staff to keep these records, much of this work must be done in the classroom.

The future will offer the capability to determine which skills and competencies should be taught to bring about desired results. We will be able to monitor teacher and administrator performance more objectively. Communities will be able to keep up with changing conditions to see if the curriculum should change.

The question is whether the ends of this record-keeping will be acceptable to teachers, students, and administrators. Teachers have not accepted performance-based evaluations in the past and will not do so unless more respect is accorded them by treating them as professionals. The first step may be to raise all teachers' salaries by 25% to a level competitive with private industry. Based on National Education Association figures, entry-level salaries for 1984 would have been $3,500 more on an average with these changes.

Information on which skills students have mastered and which they have missed—easily tabulated by computers—may also help in revising the curriculum. If more data are collected more frequently, school systems may be able to determine more precisely how and what students should be expected to perform. Standardized tests may give way to curriculum-linked tests, which, in turn, may take on a new format. This ability to collect information in large groups or in small batches does not require all schools to have the same curriculum. It simply requires all schools to match what they teach with a master list of skills or bodies of knowledge.

WE WILL KNOW MORE ABOUT LEARNING

Right now scientists are beginning to unlock information about the chemical changes that occur when learning takes place. They also know enough about the development of the brain to realize that the ability of the student in math, for example, does not increase at a steady rate. It increases in spurts. With the kind of information that can be monitored through the computer on a regular basis, scientists will be able to provide schools with information about the best times to teach various skills. The organization of the curriculum will proceed on a much more informed basis for the individual student.

WE WILL BE BETTER ABLE TO ADDRESS ISSUES OF EQUITY

Information concerning student progress and individual learning development will also allow schools to distribute their resources according to students' actual learning needs, rather than their racial, socioeconomic, or remedial status.

"SCHOOLBOOKS" WILL BE ELECTRONIC

The computer will not take the place of the book. It is rather difficult to take a computer monitor to bed with you, to admire its bindings on shelves along the living room wall, or to sit by the river on a summer's day and contemplate nature with a computer in hand.

But the disadvantages of books can be eased with the use of computer textbooks and workbooks. They can be updated rapidly. Students can write in them and teachers can correct with them quickly. Their ability to interact with students will allow the teacher to spend time creating special subroutines for those who need different approaches. If teachers have no experience with the particular learning difficulty of one of their students, they can refer a student's answers to a central diagnostic center and receive help quickly.

Basing the sequence in which skills are presented on the learning strengths of individual students will make major changes in the materials used to teach. Statewide or district-wide textbook adoptions will be replaced by lists of outcomes students are to achieve and skills they are to learn. Related tests will be a regular part of the instruction. Texas and California, states that have traditionally set standards for textbook content, will no longer be prescribing for the rest of the nation what students are to learn.

RESPONSIBILITY FOR MANAGEMENT WILL BE AT THE BUILDING LEVEL

In the 1980s, businesses may find that the middle level of managers will diminish because the computer will allow lower-level employees to gather the necessary information for making a decision, show the process that should be used to make the decision, and present the information to top-level managers on the managers' desk-top viewing screens.

In the 1990s, the role of central school administration managers in some districts may shift in much the same manner. Some districts may be able to share both top-level and middle-level administrators and will be able to do so efficiently because information-gathering and decision-making will require less time. School districts will rely more heavily on building-level management.

Instructional directors may become more commonplace and share their time among several small schools. Their responsibility will be to work with diagnostic resource managers to ensure the quality of instruction. The diagnostic resource manager will be in each classroom regularly, 2 or 3 times a month. He or she will be watching teacher performance and prescribing in-service training modules for teachers to study through telecommunication linkups with universities, the workplace, regular in-service programs, or other teachers' model classrooms. Conferences between resource managers and the instructional director will result in adjustments in student-teacher ratios, reallocations of instructional resources, and shifting of students to different schedules of instructional experiences to enrich their skills or to remedy deficiencies.

Teachers will accept the presence of these managers in their classrooms because teachers will be part of the decision-making team. Schools will be able to afford this additional layer of management because central administration personnel will be reassigned to this new management level. These highly skilled diagnostic professionals may also sell their services to various businesses as well, helping them with their training needs.

STUDENTS WILL BE SHARED BETWEEN SCHOOLS

Changes in family patterns may increase as a result of divorce and economic necessity. Electronic communication and computer-based instruction sequences may allow large numbers of students to live in the homes of both divorced parents at different times of the year. Schools will therefore need to share comparable standards and other information that will assist in instruction and in evaluating student performance, since communities in the same state or in another state will be sharing their students.

ADULTS WILL USE THE SCHOOLS AS MUCH OR MORE THAN YOUTH

Adult students will need to return to school to keep their skills up to date. All of the issues of equity, performance of staff, and appropriate instruction will need to be addressed on behalf of the adult student as well. While universities and colleges may lend resources to the public schools to carry out this adult instruction, we feel that the public schools will be the base for such instruction. Public school buildings are located conveniently and they already will have job-training programs for their youth population. If the public schools provide facilities for fast food service, babysitting, geriatric care, electronic banking, and recreational facilities, they will be more attractive than other institutions to the adult population.

WE WILL HAVE A LONGER SCHOOL DAY AND A LONGER SCHOOL YEAR

When the national report authors proposed the idea of a longer school day and year, few states responded favorably; they didn't think they had the money. But the lengthening of the school day will be an economic necessity for most schools. They will be able to use funds generated from the longer day to meet the costs of raising teacher salaries and purchasing computers. Communities will view the lengthened school day as an economic necessity as well. With dual-career households, families will need schools to provide quality preschool and late-in-the-day care, as well as job training; these families will likely be willing to pay for such services.

Once people get used to the idea of a longer school day, the traditional 9-month, 6-hour school schedule will contain the activities judged by the community to be essential. The additional time will be used for community functions, adult learning, and the expansion of young persons' creative and social skills and other activities.

While such trends as the use of electronic textbooks and diagnostic resource managers may become general practice closer to the year 2000 than the year 1990, the longer school day and year may come much sooner. The need is now. However, opinions vary on this issue. The political climate will influence how quickly or how slowly this change occurs.

It will be impossible to make the changes necessary to prepare students for the work world without more time and money. Particularly in poorer communities, schools will need to identify which services they can sell to obtain continued funding. These schools must be deeply concerned about equity and the ability of some families to pay for extra service. Initial funding for job training may be obtained from federal sources, such as the Job Training Partnership Act. It will be useful, however, for schools to offer services to adults, thereby attracting a new clientele.

RECOMMENDATIONS: CURRICULUM GOALS AND INSTRUCTIONAL DELIVERY

The reports propose a strengthening of present academic requirements to include 4 years of English, 3 years of mathematics, 3 years of science, 3 years of social studies, ½ year of computer science, and 2 years of foreign language for the college bound.

Depending on the report, emphasis is placed on science beyond the literacy stage; a foreign language for all students; an emphasis on English rather than science and math; volunteer service in the school or community; first 2 years of high school tracking all students in the same program—the final 2 being transitional for more intense academic work, career exploration, or both.

Also stressed is a strengthening of basic academic competencies.

Competencies differ from academic requirements in these reports in the sense that some skills, such as problem-solving, can be used in several courses. The recommendation is to see in what ways information can be used to form opinions and conclusions.

The reports unanimously recommend familiarity with the computer—computer literacy. In business and other areas, computer literacy has been defined as knowing how to make the computer go and performing the routine maintenance chores for the computer in much the same way we do for a car. We do not have to know how it works. We do not have to know how to write a computer program.

The reports are concerned with our human heritage in the interdependent world. This is discussed in terms of specific course(s) and competencies addressed in several courses.

Many of the same trends affecting school standards are going to affect course content. Briefly, however, the 2 most important will be our ability to collect information on students while they are learning and our ability to gear a student's pace through the curriculum to match what we know about his or her developing brain.

Right now, it is hard to say whether students who will be required to go through 1 or 2 more years of English, science, and math will learn any more in these areas than their immediate predecessors, who did not go through them. That is, will students who graduate in 1987 be able to do anything any better than those graduating in 1984 if they read and study the same kinds of books, deal with the same kinds of teachers, view the same films, write the same papers, and take the same tests? They may end up just being as bored, frustrated, or unable to remember just as great a percentage of the facts they had to memorize, spew out, and forget as the student who didn't study these areas for quite so long a time.

In other words, adding courses may or may not add skill. The essential goal is to teach students to be self-directed. This process should not begin in high school but on the first day of elementary school. As we gather more information in the classroom, we may be able to determine whether students are learning this and, if they are not, ask why not.

IN THE INFORMATION AGE, COURSE SKILLS WILL HAVE A GREATER EMPHASIS

English and mathematics are now in large measure courses of skill. The task force recommendations are concerned with the ability to express ourselves in written and oral form and to organize our thoughts. These are skills, not content. Science as well is increasingly being taught as a collection of skills rather than as so much information to be learned. Although the information provided by many courses may be irrelevant to many students' lives 5 years later, they will retain the abilities learned in these courses to gather facts, analyze them, and apply them to problems. For this reason, our traditional secondary school courses will become interdisciplinary. History and art will mix with political science and math with science. English will be used to organize our thoughts in all areas.

The National Association of Secondary School Principals has produced a chart that contrasts Directions for Education in an industrial age and an information society. It is essential today to have information readily available to the students. Schools that do not plan for this change now will produce students who cannot survive economically.

DIRECTIONS FOR EDUCATION

Goals of Education	*In an Industrial Society*	*In an Information Society*
Cognitive Goals	Basic skills	Higher-order skills and basic skills
	Specific training	Generalizable skills
	Unicultural	Global education
	Literacy	Many literacies, more than one language
Affective Goals	Large organization skills	Small-group skills
	Organization dependent	Independent,
	(Loyalty to school,	entrepreneurial
	employer)	
Curriculum	Learning simple	Interdisciplinary
	discipline skills	programs
	Standardized programs	Varied program options

Goals of Education	In an Industrial Society	In an Information Society
Curriculum (*cont.*)	Computer as a vocational skill	Computer as learning tool in all programs
Job Preparation	Single-career preparation Late skill development Distinct vocational education programs	Multiple-career preparation Early skill development Career/vocational education as integral part of educational experience
Delivery Systems		
Changing Institutional Patterns	Single district system focus Central office management Top-down, insulated decision-making Group instruction	More variety at level of individual school School-based management Bottom-up, participative decision-making Individualized instruction using technology

INTERGROUP SKILLS WILL BE IMPORTANT TO THE STUDENT

One of the most important skills of the citizen-learner will be his/her ability to network, to use the resources of other individuals. Students will be practicing this skill all through school as they refine their abilities to gather and use information. They will control a good deal of their own information-seeking as they time when they go to the computer, when they talk their results over with a problem-solving group, and when they go to the instructional designer to receive information on how to gain another perspective.

CABLE TELEVISION MAY OR MAY NOT BE AN IMPORTANT VEHICLE FOR EDUCATION

At the present time, cable television is principally a medium of news and entertainment. No one has made it a profitable source of education. Certainly, programs such as ''Nova'' and Jacques Cousteau's documentaries are educational, but they are very expensive to produce and seldom, if ever, pay their own way.

Schools must see the importance of cable TV as a medium for learning about our global business concerns as well as about other cultures. With interactive cable TV, schools might develop programs portraying other peoples and ways of looking at life and carrying debates through worldwide hookups. Students would not be passive observers, but participants. For example, business students would be able to go to business sites in their own communities or halfway across the nation through television.

Since businesses can use interactive cable TV right now to retrain adults in new technologies, adult students will probably have the advantage of cable TV first.

Interactive cable TV will be one important way for schools to address the issues of equal access to learning resources. Schools, of course, will check the percentage of homes with cable access to avoid additional equity concerns. Cable is already available in many communities. If schools cooperate in developing these resources, the cost of development will be small for any individual school district or unit—the private school, the business, the community college, or the 4-year college. But as long as schools are perceived as being contained within single buildings, the emergence of cable TV as an instructional tool will be limited.

JOB PREPARATION WILL BE A PART OF MOST COURSES

Some of the report recommendations have suggested that career exploration be included at the end of the secondary school experience. In contrast, in the future, career preparation will be accomplished largely through the processes by which we learn all through school, such as:

1. evaluation and analysis,
2. critical thinking,
3. problem-solving (including math),
4. organization and reference,
5. synthesis,
6. application to new areas,

7. creativity,

8. decision-making with incomplete information,

9. communication skills in many modes.

It may well be that when our various institutions of education get together to decide how we will address a major school population—adults—they will decide to include one year of specific-field training as part of the high school experience. We have too little information to know how likely this prospect is for the general youth population.

RECOMMENDATIONS: STAFF QUALITY AND RESPONSIBILITIES

Reports concur on the following:

- the need for more rigorous standards for teacher selection, perhaps drawing our teaching staff only from the top 25% of our college graduating classes;
- increased salaries for teachers and then incentives such as merit pay;
- increased concern for the areas of teacher shortage—math, science, and foreign languages;
- higher regard for teachers and for the profession of teaching;
- new methods to recruit and train teachers;
- quality assurance in the education of teachers;
- performance-based evaluation systems;
- limited class loads for teachers;
- career ladders for teachers and for administrators;
- the ability for teachers to transfer, without monetary penalties, to other school districts.

WE WILL BE ABLE TO MEASURE TEACHER PERFORMANCE OBJECTIVELY

The ability to measure teacher performance objectively will be increased by our ability to observe performance many times. This, of course, will be possible in part with computers but will not happen right away. Even when computers are available in a ratio of 1 computer for every 4 students, we will need a system of computer-managed instruction (CMI). With software programs that monitor the patterns of student response and teacher assistance in that response, we will be able to see how well teachers are meeting student needs.

Until the time that this capability becomes widespread, teachers may resist performance-based pay, and with good reason. We need more empirical evidence concerning the skills that make an effective teacher. We need to see teachers in many different teaching situations—with small groups, large groups, with bright students and disadvantaged students, in problem-solving groups and in creative-expression activities.

CAREER LADDERS WILL DEVELOP AROUND THE USE OF COMPUTERS

The traditional teaching job will be divided into parts. After good CMI software has been installed in schools, the information gathered on teachers' performance in a variety of situations will determine which jobs will go to which teachers. School systems will encourage this specialization because they may make money from selling various services to business interests or teachers may work part-time and sell the services themselves. Some of the new jobs may be: learning diagnostician; information gatherer for software programs; programming; curriculum designer; mental health diagnostician; evaluator of learning performances; evaluator of social skills; small-group learning facilitator; large-group learning facilitator; media production; home-based instruction designer; and home-based instruction monitor.

TEACHERS WILL SHARE JOBS

Teachers who wish to raise families, acquire additional training, or begin a transition to another career field may be able to share jobs without losing money. Until now, those who wished to teach part-time were not paid in proportion to the time they put into teaching. They lost fringe benefits. They did not gain seniority in the system at any rewarding pace.

As we approach the year 2000, however, most teachers will be job-sharing. In the first place, most people will be working a 20-hour week, while schools will be operating on a 35-hour week. Second, we will be able to judge competency on the basis of performance, not on the basis of length of time in the system. Finally, the administrative tasks that part-time teachers perform now (often without extra pay) may be handled by computers. In reality, the only teachers who will be required to work a longer workweek may be the base teachers serving the youngest students.

TEACHERS MAY COME FROM THE BUSINESS WORLD

It may not be necessary for all staff in the school to be trained in education. Educators will be part of the career team and will be able to provide the guidance necessary to assure that experts from fields outside of education will present their materials effectively. (The educator of the future will have extensive experience with such topics as brain development chemistry, learning environment alternatives, cognitive and psychosomatic evaluation, and affective development.)

TEACHERS MAY WORK IN THE BUSINESS WORLD

Businesses may find it necessary to hire educators as consultants as they need periodically to organize new technological material for retraining workers.

TEACHERS' UNIONS WILL DIMINISH

Unions flourish where workers have no access to other, comparable job opportunities. With career ladders and crossovers between the teaching world and business, other options exist for competent teachers.

But what happens to teachers who are not competent? There will be a much smaller percentage of these because of the same forces that allow opportunity for competent teachers. Incompetency in teaching may be much more a product of the gargantuan expectations we have of teachers. If we divide up the teaching tasks, we are much more likely to find areas where expertise may be exhibited.

RECOMMENDATIONS: ADMINISTRATIVE, FEDERAL, STATE, AND LOCAL RESPONSIBILITIES

A large number of recommendations involve actions to be carried out by the federal government. That is a reflection of our national interest in quality education. However, the federal government cannot be responsible for making actual necessary changes in the schools. Schools retain this ultimate responsibility but the emphasis in these reports on the federal role is understandable. In the first place, the federal government provided funding for 4 of the major studies. Additionally, one entire report was written about the federal government's role. An independent research foundation, the Twentieth Century Fund, created a task force composed of 12 members representing postsecondary institutions, state departments of education, local school districts, and the academic community. But the group started from the assumption that the federal government has the responsibility to help overcome the unevenness of state efforts and to assure quality and equity in education.

Within this context, the recommendations for federal government action seem limited—even though the list is long and important. The federal government should do research, ensure equity, fund incentives, and set images to define benefits for the nation as a whole in high-quality education.

The same limited role is defined for the state by the various reports. The state should fund incentives and reward teacher excellence. It should list priorities.

But action should occur predominantly at the local level.

The following is a list of recommendations for federal government action:

- emphasize the need for better education and better schools for all students;
- provide incentives that promote a high English proficiency in all schools;
- provide the opportunity to all students to study a foreign language;
- promote going beyond basic scientific literacy;
- provide advanced training in math and science;

- focus aid on school districts with large numbers of immigrant or poor children;
- provide data collection and research on model programs for the year 2000;
- provide for alternative academies for students who are failing;
- encourage merit-based pay;
- reward excellence in teaching through national fellowships.

The state government should:

- examine the possible benefits of a longer school day and longer school year;
- develop immediate plans for improving education;
- create broader and more effective partnerships for improving education, especially with business leaders;
- assure more effective use of existing resources;
- place a higher priority on improving education statewide;
- continue a role in helping to guarantee access for disadvantaged;
- provide research and development;
- stimulate creative ways to organize and staff schools;
- assure the availability of alternative curricular designs and pedagogical procedures.

Local districts should:

- provide leadership for improvement efforts;
- obtain needed funds;
- decentralize authority to the local school site;
- stimulate long-range planning in each school;
- articulate elementary, middle, and senior high schools;
- divide large secondary schools into smaller units.

Research is needed at all levels on more effective ways of teaching, especially for those students who do not succeed traditionally.

Strangely, the conservative cast of these suggestions—placing responsibility on local districts and local buildings instead of the other levels of government—fits two major trends, the increased activity of the citizen in government at the local level and the development of information networks at the level where action is to be implemented.

CITIZENS WILL INCREASE THEIR POLITICAL ACTIVITY AT THE LOCAL LEVEL

Citizens' political activity at the local level will increase because of the growing skepticism of the public toward government in general— a government far removed from their own supervision and input.

Communities may become much more involved in school planning and the actual implementation of the programs. Planners who recognize the immensity of their tasks in educating and/or retraining whole populations on a lifelong basis will welcome this activity.

Those schools that do not plan for their communities' partnerships, that limit community involvement to activities such as PTA meetings and newsletters—may find that they cannot survive. Relationships must become stronger and more broadly based to ensure the future of the community.

INFORMATION NETWORKS WILL CREATE HORIZONTAL LINES OF POWER

As local groups plan for their educational goals, they will need to call on resources and information outside of their community. This help may not be provided by the state or the federal government to any great extent. However, schools may be able to generate revenues by providing services to businesses, workers, parents, and other groups at the community level.

The organizations that will have the money are business groups and perhaps the local school itself as it begins to generate income through offering service to business.

That means that businesses from one community will communicate with those in another community. Schools will communicate from one town to the next; and there will be business/school hookups.

Those schools and businesses that provide greater resource pools will become more powerful. They will have an increased voice in government and in their ability to attract even greater resources.

APPENDIX B:

THE NATIONAL EDUCATION REFORM REPORTS

Education is in the national spotlight. Several major reports on education have helped to put it there. As a result of this increased attention, schools have an opportunity to rally their communities to make schools even more effective and to build support for quality education. The American Association of School Administrators, for example, has recommended that schools not be defensive about the recommendations, but to give them every consideration to see if further action is needed.

The national education reform reports have made hundreds of comments and recommendations for improving education. The major federal government report, *A Nation at Risk*, asks that states convene panels to do the same, outlining broad policy statements. The school districts are asked to develop action plans.

The reports are a useful starting point. Even though they barely mention how to deal with students not planning to attend college or how our adult population will need to be reeducated and retrained every 5 to 10 years, the recommendations do underscore the need to make all students proficient in science, technology, and communication. But the recommendations need to be digested and put into a format that will give planners an overview of the points that need attention.

A number of educational organizations have developed suggestions for turning recommendations into action. For example, the AASA has produced a workbook titled *Excellence in Our Schools . . . Making It Happen.* That publication clusters the hundreds of recommendations into 7 operational components: goals and curriculum priorities; standards, expectations, and requirements; instructional content and process; school organization and instructional delivery; instructional time; using available resources; and staff roles, responsibilities, and rewards. AASA, in this workbook, suggests that people from the school and community get together in planning sessions to examine these questions:

- What are we doing now in our schools that contributes to dealing effectively with this set of recommendations?
- What could we or should we be doing to deal with this set of recommendations?
- What specific steps or plan of action will we follow to get from where we are to where we would like to be?

The National School Public Relations Association (NSPRA) has developed a chart showing the categories of recommendations found in each of several reports. That chart appears after these notes.

NOTES ABOUT THE CHARTS

Education recently has been the subject of nearly 30 major national reports and countless state and local ones. All carried recommendations for improving American education. Many suggestions were similar, but each report offered its own unique view of the situation, adding new issues to the discussions or avoiding those its authors deemed less important.

The accompanying chart highlights the areas of consensus and the common themes in the national reports that have gotten the most attention and thus are likely to have the largest impact on educational reform. The chart is not presented as a definitive summary of everything touched on in the reports, nor does it delineate what is not discussed. Each report is rich in details and nuances and differences of philosophy that can only be gleaned by an individual reading. While it can be said, for example, that certain studies recommended changes in vocational education classes, the chart cannot show the gamut of the recommendations, which ranged from eliminating vocational education altogether to making work experience a part of every student's curriculum.

Other reports present both recommendations and dissenting views, making them difficult to summarize. Some, such as Ernest Boyer's *High School*, John Goodlad's *A Place Called School*, and Ted Sizer's *Horace's Compromise*, based on field work and personal perspectives, are loaded with observations about schooling. Mortimer Adler's *Paideia Proposal* presents more of a philosophy of education than a set of steps toward improvement.

Some of the reports are devoted to one aspect of education or were published by groups with a specific interest. *America's Competitive Challenge*, for example, dealt mostly with higher education as it relates to the nation's competitive position in the world economy. *Education for Tomorrow's Jobs* is an attempt to make up for what its authors deemed a lack of attention to vocational studies in the other reports.

The chart, therefore, should be taken as a broad overview of major areas of agreement and as a starting point to guide you to the various individual reports.

CURRICULUM/STANDARDS	REVISE CURRICULUM	STRENGTHEN REQUIREMENTS: – ENGLISH	– MATH	– SCIENCE	– SOCIAL STUDIES	– TECHNOLOGY/COMPUTER SCIENCE	– FOREIGN LANGUAGES	– ART, MUSIC	– PHYSICAL EDUCATION
A NATION AT RISK	●	●	●	●	●	●	●	●	
ACTION FOR EXCELLENCE	●	●	●	●	●	●			
MAKING THE GRADE		●	●	●	●	●	●		
ACADEMIC PREPARATION FOR COLLEGE	●	●	●	●	●	●	●	●	
A PLACE CALLED SCHOOL		●	●	●	●	●		●	●
HIGH SCHOOL	●	●	●	●	●	●	●	●	●
HORACE'S COMPROMISE	●								
EDUCATING AMERICANS FOR THE 21ST CENTURY	●		●	●	●	●			
AMERICA'S COMPETITIVE CHALLENGE									
EDUCATION FOR TOMORROW'S JOBS									
THE PAIDEIA PROPOSAL	●	●	●	●	●			●	●
HIGH SCHOOLS AND THE CHANGING WORKPLACE		●	●	●	●	●			
AN OPEN LETTER TO AMERICA	●								
MEETING THE NEED FOR QUALITY: ACTION IN THE SOUTH			●	●					

Prepared by the editors of *Education USA*,
National School Public Relations Assn., 1984

EDUCATION REFORM REPORTS

Revise Vocational/Work Courses	Begin Education Earlier	Offer Special Help for Gifted and Talented	Offer Special Help for Slow Learners	Set Core Curriculum	Incorporate Outside Learning Opportunities	Emphasize Reasoning Skills	Upgrade/Improve Textbooks	Eliminate Tracking/Group by Mastery	Raise College Admissions Standards	Expect More of Students	Test for Promotion/Graduation	Increase Discipline	Assign More Homework
●		●	●			●	●	●	●		●	●	●
		●	●	●		●	●	●	●	●	●	●	●
			●	●									
						●					●		
●	●	●	●	●		●		●		●	●		
●		●	●	●	●			●	●	●			
●				●		●		●		●			
		●	●		●	●	●		●	●	●	●	●
								●					
●													
●	●		●			●		●		●		●	
●					●	●				●	●	●	
	●	●	●			●				●	●	●	
●													

MAJOR RECOMMENDATIONS OF

	TEACHING								ORGANIZATION
	Raise Salaries	Set Career Incentives	Strengthen Teacher Education	Offer Incentives to Attract	Recognize Outstanding Teachers	Strengthen Evaluation/Testing	Provide More Control/Fewer Administrative Burdens	Improve Math/Science Training/Teaching	
A Nation at Risk	•	•	•		•	•	•	•	
Action for Excellence	•	•	•	•	•	•	•	•	
Making the Grade	•	•		•	•			•	
Academic Preparation for College									
A Place Called School		•	•			•			
High School	•	•	•	•	•	•	•	•	
Horace's Compromise	•						•		
Educating Americans for the 21st Century	•	•	•	•	•	•	•	•	
America's Competitive Challenge									•
Education for Tomorrow's Jobs									
The Paideia Proposal	•		•	•			•		
High Schools and the Changing Workplace									
An Open Letter to America	•		•			•	•		
Meeting the Need for Quality: Action in the South				•	•	•	•		

Prepared by the editors of *Education USA*,
National School Public Relations Assn., 1984

EDUCATION REFORM REPORTS (cont.)

Improve School Environment/Working Conditions	Improve School Leadership/Management	Lengthen School Day/Year	Use Existing School Time Better	Reduce Class/School Size	Increase Parent Involvement	Increase Business/Community Involvement	Form School/College Links	Governance/Funding Responsibility: – Local	– State	Main Federal Role Cited As: – Research	– Equity/Civil Rights	– Funding Specific Projects	– Information/Data Collection	– Identification of National Initiatives	– Teacher Training/Support
	•	•	•		•	•	•	•	•	•	•	•	•	•	•
	•	•	•	•		•		•	•	•	•	•	•	•	
								•		•	•	•	•	•	•
							•								
•	•		•	•											
•	•		•	•	•	•	•		•	•		•			•
•	•	•	•	•		•	•	•	•	•	•	•	•	•	•
						•	•					•			
						•						•			
	•													•	
						•	•								•
•	•			•		•			•	•	•	•	•		
	•						•								

WHERE TO FIND THE REPORTS

Academic Preparation for College: What Students Need to Know and Be Able to Do, the College Board, Office of Academic Affairs, 888 5th Ave., NYC 10106; single copies free, multiple copies in packages of 20 for $20. (1984)

Action for Excellence: A Comprehensive Plan to Improve Our Nation's Schools, Education Commission of the States, Suite 300, 1860 Lincoln St., Denver, CO 80295; $5. (1983)

Making the Grade, The Twentieth Century Fund, 41 E. 70th St., NYC 10021; $6. (1983)

A Nation at Risk: The Imperative for Educational Reform, Supt. of Documents, U.S. Govt. Printing Office, Washington, DC 20402, (#065-000-00177-2); $4.50. (1983)

A Place Called School, (John I. Goodlad), McGraw-Hill Book Co., Princeton Rd., Hightstown, NJ 08520; $18.95. (1984)

High School: A Report on Secondary Education in America, (Ernest L. Boyer), Harper & Row, 10 E. 53rd St., NYC 10022; $15. (1983)

America's Competitive Challenge: The Need for a National Response, Business-Higher Education Forum, Suite 800, One Dupont Circle NW, Washington, DC 20036; $17.50. (1983)

Meeting the Need for Quality: Action in the South, Southern Regional Education Board, 1340 Spring St. NW, Atlanta, GA 30309; $3. (1983)

Educating Americans for the 21st Century, National Science Board, National Science Foundation, Washington, DC 20550; no charge. (1983)

Education for Tomorrow's Jobs, National Academy Press, 2101 Constitution Avenue, NW, Washington, DC 20418; $10.50. (1983)

High Schools and the Changing Workplace, National Academy Press, 2101 Constitution Avenue, NW, Washington, DC 20418; $5.25. (1984)

Horace's Compromise: The Dilemma of the American High School, (Theodore R. Sizer), Houghton Mifflin Company, Two Park Street, Boston, MA 02108; $16.95. (1984)

The Paideia Proposal, (Mortimer J. Adler), Macmillan Publishing Company, 866 Third Avenue, New York, NY 10002; $2.95. (1982)

An Open Letter to America on Schools, Students, and Tomorrow, National Education Association, 1201 16th Street, NW, Washington, DC 20036; no charge. (1984)

WHAT'S MISSING FROM THE NATIONAL EDUCATION REFORM REPORTS? (VIEWS FROM EDUCATORS AND LEGISLATORS)*

Some curriculum people object to the way most of the commissions and studies propose achieving excellence. "We are caught in the trap of proposing expectations for students that are highly appealing to the public," said Gordon Cawelti, executive director of the Association for Supervision and Curriculum Development. "But the reports leave out an understanding of learning. . . . Someone is going to get hurt." (Issue dated 3/19/84*)

Both Daniel Tanner of Rutgers University and Gerald Firth of the University of Georgia noted that the reports ignore vocational education. Firth feels we are "headed toward strictly academic high schools." Mary Ann Raywid of Hofstra University believes the real agenda of some of the reports is "standardization," which ignores the existence of "multiple intelligences, multiple excellences." (3/19/84)

Glen Harvey of WGH Associates of Bethesda, Maryland, has charged the National Commission on Excellence in Education specifically with ignoring research that could tell schools how to make improvements. The commission, he added, "has no accountability for seeing its recommendations translated into practice." (4/30/84)

Harold Howe II, former U.S. Commissioner of Education, listed concerns which he sees developing as a result of hearings throughout

---

*Excerpted from *Education USA*, published by the National School Public Relations Association.

the country on the effect of the excellence movement on disadvantaged children. Motivation of students was cited by Howe as "the major missing component" of the reports. (5/7/84)

"The carrot is more effective than the stick. If you're going to change things, you must allocate funds," said Delaware Governor Pierre du Pont IV, new Education Commission of the States chairperson. Some recommendations are so costly they are prohibitive, he said, and urged that state and federal grant funds reimburse school districts that adopt educational improvement programs. Schools need action, not more reports, he added. (8/1/83)

States that want to implement improvements recommended by the National Commission on Excellence in Education will have to take a close look at their finance systems, said John Augenblick, director of the ECS Education Finance Center. States already provide 50% of all school revenues and 71% of new revenues. They will therefore "be in a position, through their school finance systems, to influence school district behavior," Augenblick noted. Robert Teeter, president of Market Opinion Research of Michigan, said polls show 50–70% of people would pay higher taxes if they believe educational quality is improving. "Accountability and competence" rather than "accessibility and quantity" are big issues with voters today, he said. (8/1/83)

The National Commission of Excellence in Education recommends much tougher standards in schools, but it was not specific about increased funding. There was an early consensus in commission discussions against a strong federal role, said Yvonne Larson, former president of the San Diego school board. The local and state tax base should be the source of funding for education, and "when people see improvements taking place," they will support the schools, she said. (4/18/83)

Local school officials have found themselves battling over control and funding with state and federal education authorities in the wake of the National Commission on Excellence in Education's reports. Joan Parent, National School Boards Association president for 1983, says the reports present a changing role for local school boards. Now they are forerunners in making changes and not simply reactors to state and federal officials' demands. But a "meshing of public opinion" is needed for school boards to take the lead. Tom Chappelear, a member of the Greenville, SC, board feels that "local boards like to operate with guidelines from the state and not be told what or how to teach." "School boards should put the goal out there, and local boards should have the choice," he says. (5/2/83)

Proposed reforms are costly to implement, says Joy Korologos, a Fairfax County, Virginia, school board member. Her board has figured it will take $11 million extra to lengthen the school year, $12 million to begin a career ladder for teachers and $3 million to improve school science labs. The district cannot begin improvements without assurance that revenues won't dry up, she said. "It will damage our credibility to put in more changes than we can afford." (12/19/84)

"The most glaring omission [in the various reports on educational reform] is any detailed estimate of . . . costs and how they are to be met," stated Harold Howe II in the November *Phi Delta Kappan*. He also has a "nagging concern" that the economic goals will push aside other equally important ones. (11/14/83)

"Public willingness to support education [reforms] is tied to results in the classroom," said Florida Governor Bob Graham. The problem will be how to make improvements fast enough to convince the public that something is being done while at the same time avoiding "quick fixes" that don't do the job effectively in the long run. (12/19/83)

Efforts to upgrade public schools may be undermined if colleges and universities fail to raise standards. "Colleges and universities have accommodated the decline by offering remedial courses," claims David Gardner, who chaired the National Commission on Excellence in Education. As president of the University of Utah, Gardner pushed to eliminate remedial courses for credit, forcing students to pay extra for the noncredit courses. (11/14/83)

Senator Lowell Weicker, as head of an appropriations subcommittee, is in a key position with regard to the National Commission on Excellence in Education's report's basic recommendations. "We want all this excellence," he mused. "Someone's got to pay for it." (5/9/83)

During the March 1984 annual conference of the American Education Finance Association, conferees were told repeatedly that the cost of excellence is high. Whether school districts decide to improve or innovate, more money is needed. (3/26/84)

Education for Tomorrow's Jobs lists access to employment positions as a concern; however, none of its recommendations addresses access for women. (11/14/83)

Recent reports on education have paid little attention to elementary schools, but when 40 education leaders met in Racine, Wisconsin, in September of 1983, they were given the reason. The elementary schools weren't left out of the reports because of unimportance; rather, it was because it was time to turn the focus away from elementary education. Tom Tomlinson, director of research for the National Commission on Excellence in Education, explains that in the past 25 years, much research has been done in elementary education. Commissioners were concerned about a "loss of tone" in high schools and colleges, he said. Ernest Boyer, president of the Carnegie Foundation for the Advancement of Teaching, said he looked at secondary schools in his study because they are "the sickest." (9/26/83)

A 1984 survey of principals showed a reluctance to increase time spent in school and a preference for making better use of existing schedules. 1,208 principals ranked reforms typically recommended by major studies, such as "A Nation at Risk," at the bottom of 24 widely suggested reforms, said James Albrecht, education administration professor at the University of Northern Iowa. This raises questions about how effective many of the reforms will be if principals do not support them. Adds Albrecht, "The principal is critical in implementing any program if it is going to succeed." (7/16/84)

John Goodlad cautions against "more of the same" in response to the National Commission on Excellence in Education's recommendation of a longer school day and year. Polk and Halifax school districts in North Carolina chose a middle ground. After increasing their school day to 7 hours and adding 20 days to their year, officials also changed some of the ways they used time. Halifax concentrated on instruction and eliminated distractions. "I suspect one major factor is that we stopped interrupting classes," said Halifax superintendent James Clarke. "Giving students 'more of the same' won't help unless the 'same' is good," noted Polk superintendent Jim Benfield. (6/25/84)

Allan Odden, former director of Educational Commission of the States's Education Finance Center, warns, "A lot of money will be spent, and the impact will not be too great." Initially, higher teachers' salaries will cost about $20 billion nationally but probably won't improve the quality of education. They simply are ''more of what you've got,'' he said. (2/27/84)

Many state reform programs are in progress, not just beginning. ''We're so far ahead of that [the excellence commission report] that we haven't done a darn thing in direct response to it,'' candidly commented Jack Lynch, coordinator of communication services for the Mississippi State Department of Education. Dave Bolger, Arizona assistant to the superintendent, said ''the state's push toward excellence was not motivated by the commission report. . . . However, it has elevated dialogue to the national level . . . creating an opportunity that will enable us to move faster.'' (9/5/84)

Many high school seniors are wondering what all the fuss is about. They have earned an average of 22.4 credits altogether, more than most of the new standards set by states. Seniors fall short in only two areas, foreign languages and computer sciences. The 1984 *Condition of Education*, an annual publication of the United States Department of Education, attributes these findings to the performances of certain subgroups. Catholic school students in particular tend to be above the minimum standards being set in many states. (5/4/84)

Susan Fuhrman of the Eagleton Institute of Politics at Rutgers University says the education reform hoopla may be creating some unrealistic expectations among the general public. ''Education reform is a long, slow and complex process. It may be five to ten years before we see an improvement in test scores,'' she said. Legislators should set interim goals, such as increasing attendance and enrollment in more difficult classes, before looking for test-score results. Fuhrman also warned about the consequences of tightening standards. Increasing graduation requirements may lead to higher numbers of dropouts. (7/30/84)

Although the Commission reports on education recommended a more challenging curriculum, there was no real consensus on what measures would best achieve that goal, according to the 1983 *Condition of Education* report. More than 1 in 5 program heads reported ''major adverse effects'' on their schools from increased standards. (6/20/84)

In Ted Sizer's *Horace's Compromise*, the ''complexity and subtlety'' of teaching is emphasized. Although Sizer explores many aspects of teaching, including what is taught and how it is taught, he dismisses physical education as being neither physical nor educational for most students and says that the best vocational education is on-site job training. Furthermore, attaching numbers—of hours, of credits—to educational change avoids the real issues, Sizer insists. They are important, but "secondary to issues of attitude." (1/30/84).

ACKNOWLEDGMENTS

The authors are deeply indebted to the American Association of School Administrators (AASA) for the opportunity to develop a statement to the general public about our future schools. It is difficult to reflect the best thinking of our times on how schools may change. We doubt we could have accomplished the goal they set before us without their ongoing support. AASA Executive Director, Dr. Paul B. Salmon, and the AASA staff have strengthened the content of this publication through their insights and critical comment.

Beyond the continuous support from AASA, we had technical assistance from the Education Research Service data analysis and library personnel; our liaison there was Nancy Protheroe, who had a sure feel for providing us with practical information. Many people assisted us unselfishly, giving their time to supply us with a more sensitive appreciation of the field we were examining: Jane Quinn, the Executive Director of Girls Clubs of America; Thelma Petrilak, Supervisor, Fairfax County Office of Aging and a nationally recognized authority on senior issues; Dan Meranda, Executive Director of the National School Volunteers Association; Dr. Erwin Flaxman, Director of the Clearinghouse on Urban Education, and Dr. Denny Taylor of Columbia Teachers College; Dr. Grace Burkart, Editor of the *ESP* (English For Special Purposes) *Journal*; Marge Crawford of the Cooperative Educational Service Agency 19 in Wisconsin, who advised us on school/business partnerships; Edward Rodriguez, supervisor in GM Truck and Coach Division; Hilda Uribe of Future Computing, Inc., for assistance on future projections in the home computer market; the Educational Commission of the States; the research office of the National Educational Association; the Bilingual Education Clearinghouse; Dr. Warren Eisenhower, Personnel Director, and Dr. Mary Ann Lecos, Curriculum Director of Fairfax County (Virginia) Public Schools.

Countless hours have been contributed by Dr. John Wherry, Executive Director of the National School Public Relations Association, and by Richard Bagin, Virginia Ross, Anne Lewis, and Sherry Freeland, who compiled the overview chart of the national education reform reports.

Special gratitude is felt for the assistance of Dr. Jesse Soriano, Assistant Secretary of the Office of Bilingual Education and Minority Language Affairs, for assisting us with data from his office and from the offices for Civil Rights and the National Commission on Educational Excellence.

For the patience, hard work, and unrelenting support of Idali Feliciano, we owe much. We thank Kristen Amundson for the difficult task of blending points of view in the final draft. For proofreading and level-headed comment, we thank Catherine Acton, Barbara Weir, and Charles McFadden of the Forecasting International staff. For the often thankless tasks of typing, editing, and organizing, we thank Susan McGuirk and Donna Siljander.

INDEX

Academic Preparation for College, 148–151, 152
Action for Excellence, 148–151, 152
Adler, Mortimer, 147, 148–151, 153
Adopt-a-school program, 86
Adult education programs, 50t
Adult students, 6, 15, 16, 39, 132
Albrecht, James, 156
America's Competitive Challenge, 147, 148–151, 152
Aquarian Conspiracy, The (Ferguson), 101
Augenblick, John, 154
Automobile industry, retraining programs for, 88

Benfield, Jim, 156
Bilingual education research, 75
Birth rate, 40
Blacks:
in job market, 9–10
(*See also* Minorities)
Bolger, Dave, 157
Boyer, Ernest, 147, 148–151, 152, 156
Buffington, Perry, 108

Business:
careers for teachers in, 20, 140
day care programs of, 68
entrepreneurship in, 29
and foreign competition, 26
foreign language needs of, 43, 75
home-based, 29–30
job skill requirements of, 65t, 89–90
in job training, 28
minority-owned, 53t
in school funding, 81, 86–87
school partnership with, 85–88, 95, 96
spin-off companies, 28–29
and tax base, 80
teleconferencing in, 34–35
women-owned, 59t, 60t
work at home option, 40–41, 42

Cable television:
as instructional tool, 16, 29, 136–137
social impact of, 42
Career preparation, 137–138
Cawelti, Gordon, 153

Chappelear, Tom, 154–155
Child care. (*see* Day care)
Child custody:
    arrangements, 62t
    joint, and dual school attendance,
        40, 41–42, 69, 132
Clarke, James, 156
Class size, 99–101
College and universities:
    age of students in, 23
    standards in, 155
    teacher education in, 110, 115–116,
        118, 119
    technological education in, 26
Coming Crisis in Teaching, The, 110–
    111
Computer(s):
    administrative tasks of, 33
    homework drill on, 124
    literacy, 134
    in peer teaching, 100
    social impact of, 42–43
    software for, 17, 19, 33
    teacher performance evaluation,
        138–139
    textbooks, 130
    (*See also* Technology)
Computer-based instruction:
    and educational equity, 10
    equipment for, 19–20, 32
    in home, 16–17
    in job training, 20
    software for, 17, 19
    in writing curriculum, 103
Condition of Education 1984, 157
Conference Board, 86
Creativity:
    computers and, 43
    intelligence and, 9, 108
    stages of, 108
Curriculum:
    basic core-course structure, 102–
        104
    career preparation in, 137–138
    community input in, 11
    computer-managed design, 104–105
    constraints on, 102

course skills in, 135–136
    data collection for, 128–129
    for expanded school year, 96
    for gifted students, 108
    goals of, 133–134
    and learning process, 129–130
    technology and, 107
    writing, 103

Day care:
    arrangements, 61t
    entrepreneur services in, 41
    in schools, 68–69, 94
Diagnostic resource managers, 131
Disabled people, work at home option
    for, 42
Displaced workers, 27, 28, 68
Divorce:
    and family life, 61t, 62t
        impact on schools, 40, 41–42,
            69, 132
    rate, 40
Dropouts:
    minorities, 74
    preventive measures for, 13
Du Pont, Pierre, IV, 154

Early childhood education, 76
*Educating Americans for the 21st
    Century*, 148–151, 152
Education for Tomorrow's Jobs, 147,
    148–151, 152, 155–156
Education reform:
    attitude of principals to, 156
    issues in, 5–13
Education reform reports, national:
    criticism of, 153–158
    focus on college bound, 6
    limitations of, 123–126
    ordering copies of, 152–153
    recommendations of, 127–143,
        145–146
    summarized, 146–151
"Electronic cottage," 29–30, 40–
    41

Elementary education, in national
reports, 156
Employment (*see* Job(s))
Entrepreneurs:
in day care services, 41
displaced workers as, 28
training program for, 29
*Excellence in Our Schools . . .
Making It Happen*, 127, 146

Family:
changes in, 40–42, 61t, 62t, 69–70,
132
school as resource center for, 70
Federal government:
education funds of, 14, 79
for disadvantaged, 73
national reports on role of, 141–142
Ferguson, Marilyn, 101
Firth, Gerald, 153
Flexible work schedules, 21
Foreign language instruction, 39, 43,
75
Fuhrman, Susan, 157

Gardner, David, 155
Goldhar, Joel, 25
Goodlad, John, 147, 148–151, 152,
156
Graham, Bob, 155
"Graying of America," 39

Harvey, Glen, 153
High School (Boyer), 147, 148–151,
152
*High Schools and the Changing
Workplace*, 89, 148–151, 152
Hispanics:
education level of, 73–74
geographical distribution of, 54t
voter turnout for, 54t
(*See also* Minorities)
Home:
language, instruction in, 9, 75

learning, 12–13, 17, 29–30, 32,
35–36, 96
workplace, 12, 29–30
for disabled, 42
for women, 40–41
Homemakers, schools as employers
of, 71
Homework, 124
Horace's Compromise (Sizer), 147,
148–151, 153, 157–158
Howe, Harold, II, 153–154, 155

Imig, David, 113
Individual education plans (IEPs), 17,
75, 105–106
Inner-city schools, technology for,
23–24
Instructional directors, 131
Intelligence, and creativity, 9, 108
Internship, teacher, 21

Job(s):
market:
blacks in, 9–10
displaced worker in, 8, 27, 28,
68
retraining for, 6, 27
technical training for, 6, 26
placement programs, 71, 74
retraining, 6, 27, 76, 82, 87–88
sharing, by teachers, 100, 116,
139–140
skills:
business requirements for, 65t,
89–90
entrepreneurial, 29
foreign language, 43, 75
obsolescence of, 8
training. (*see* Training programs)
Johns Hopkins University, 8, 9–10

Kerr, Clark, 30
Korologos, Joy, 155

Labor force:
  age of, 37
  minorities in, 38
  women in. (*see* Women, in labor
    force)
Larson, Yvonne, 154
Learning process, 129–130
Lifestyle of future:
  demographic change and, 37–40
  family patterns in, 40–42, 61t, 62t,
    132
  impact of technology on, 42–43
Literacy:
  basic, 6–7
  school programs, 76
  technological, 115–116, 134
Lynch, Jack, 157

Making the Grade, 148–151, 152
Martin, John Henry, 103
Mathematics instruction, 26
*Meeting the Need for Quality: Action
  in the South*, 148–151, 152
Merit-pay plans, 12, 113–114
Minimum competencies, 18
Minorities:
  business ownership by, 53t
  education level of, 73–74
  English proficiency of, 52t
  and home language instruction, 9
  in labor force, 38
  below poverty level, 51t
  school enrollment of, 50t
  senior citizen population of, 46t
  special programs for, 75–76
  unemployment rate of, 74

Nation at Risk, A, 5, 145, 148–151,
  152, 156
Nation Responds, A, 5
National Commission on Excellence in
  Education, 153, 154, 155
National education reform reports
  (*see* Education reform reports,
  national)

Odden, Allan, 156
*Open Letter to America on Schools,
  Students and Tomorrow, An*,
  148–151, 153

Paideia Proposal (Adler), 147, 148–
  151, 153
Parent, Joan, 154
Parents:
  divorced and single working
    parents, 12
  in joint custody arrangements, 40,
    41–42, 69, 132
  purchase of technology by, 10, 31,
    34
  volunteers, 11–12
Peer teaching, 100
Place Called School, A (Goodlad),
  147, 148–151, 152
Political power:
  of senior citizen, 39
  and voter turnout, 49t
  and voting blocs, 55t
  of women, 38, 39, 56t–57t
Population characteristics, 44t–60t
  future, 37–40
Poverty rate, 38, 48t
Principals, and education reform, 156
Professions, women in, 66–67

Rand report, on teaching profession,
  110–111
Ravitch, Diane, 24
Raywid, Mary Ann, 153
Retraining programs, 6, 27, 76, 82,
  86–88

SAT scores, for entering teachers, 113
School boards, 154–155
Schools:
  available technology in, 30, 31, 32
  costs of, 78–79, 83, 155
  funding:
    by business, 81, 86–87

Schools (*cont.*):
  entrepreneurial approach to, 84,
    106
  federal grants, 14, 79
  for retraining programs, 82
  sources of, 62t, 154
  from state budget, 79–80
  tax base and, 80
  of technology, 34
  physical plants, 64t, 78
  population decline, 37, 44t
  public support for, 63t, 121, 154,
    155
  standards, 5–6
Schools of future:
  administration of, 131
  adult students in, 6, 15, 16, 39,
    132
  building shortage and surplus in,
    39–40
  business cooperation with, 85–88,
    95, 96
  cable television in, 136–137
  community involvement in, 10–11,
    143
  computer-based instruction in:
    and educational equality, 10
    equipment for, 19–20, 32
    in home, 16–17
    in job training, 20
    software for, 17, 19
    in writing curriculum, 103
  current trends and, 14–15
  day care programs in, 68–69
  design of, 31–32
  dropout prevention in, 13
  educational equality in, 10, 80–82,
    126
  employment services of, 71
    for minorities, 74
  extended school day and year, 15–
    16, 92–97, 132–133, 156
  as family center, 70
  and family pattern changes, 12, 40,
    41–42, 69, 132
  federal role in, 141–142
  foreign language instruction in, 39

  gifted students in, 107–108
  influence of women on, 39
  inner-city, 23–24
  job training in, 6, 20, 28, 106
    for college-bound student, 22–23
    entrepreneurial skills in, 29
    school-guided part-time work,
      7–8
  minority instruction applications to,
    75–76
  pupil-teacher ratio, 99–101
  retraining programs in, 6, 27, 76,
    82, 86–87
  sociological forces and, 25–26
  student standards in, 105–106, 124–
    125
  textbooks in, 33–34
  volunteer programs in, 11–12, 67,
    100, 116
  (*See also* Curriculum; Students;
    Teachers)
Science instruction, 26
Senior citizens:
  and demographic shifts, 37–38
  political power of, 39
  in population, 44t, 45t
    by age and sex, 47t
    income of, 49t
    poverty rate for, 48t
  as students, 14
  in volunteer programs, 11–12, 100
Single-parent family, 12, 61t
Sizer, Ted, 147, 148–151, 153, 157–
  158
Software, development of, 17, 19, 33
States:
  education funds of, 79–80
  educational equity in, 80–81
  national education reform reports
    on, 142
  teacher pay in, 111–113
Students:
  categorization of, 9
  college-bound, 22–23
  dropouts, 13
  gifted and talented, 107–108
  group assignment of, 18–19

Students *(cont.)*:
  home learning by, 12–13, 17, 29–
    30, 32, 35–36
  individual education plan (IEP) for,
    17
  intergroup skills of, 69–70, 136
  in joint custody arrangements, 40,
    41–42, 69, 132
  minimum competencies of, 18
  standards for, 105–106, 124–125
  -teacher ratio, 99–101
Sun Belt:
  migration to, 38
  school shortages in, 39, 40

Tanner, Daniel, 153
Teachers:
  business careers for, 20, 140
  from business world, 21, 140
  education programs for, 110, 115–
    116, 118, 119
  flexible work schedule for, 21
  internships, 21
  job-sharing by, 100, 116, 139–140
  performance evaluation of, 21,
    138–139
  -pupil ratio, 99–101
  quality of, 26, 111, 113, 124
  salaries of, 15, 20, 129, 156–157
    increases in, 114–115
    merit-pay plan, 12, 113–114
    by state, 111–113
  science and mathematics, 26
  in software development, 17, 19,
    33
  staff development programs for,
    118
  status in year 2000, 117, 119
  student assignment to, 18–19
  in teaching-teams, 17, 21
  teleconferencing opportunities for,
    35
  unions, 118, 119, 140
Technology:
  availability of, 30–31
  and curriculum, 107
  funding for, 34

for inner city schools, 23–24
  product life cycles in, 25
  and school change, 25–26
  and school design, 31–32
  social impact of, 42–43
  standard literacy in, 115–116, 134
  U.S. leadership in, 26
  (*See also* Computer(s); Computer-
    based instruction)
Teeter, Robert, 154
Teleconferencing, 34–35
Television (*see* Cable television)
Textbooks:
  computer, 130
  teacher-set criteria for, 33
Tomlinson, Tom, 156
Training programs, 6, 106
  business input, 28
  for college-bound student, 22–23
  computer simulations in, 20
  entrepreneurial skills in, 29
  school-guided part-time work, 7–8,
    13
Translation machines, 43

Unemployment, 74
Universities (*see* Colleges and
    universities)
University of New Hampshire, teacher
    education program at, 115
University of Texas, literacy survey
    of, 7

Vocational education (*see* Retraining
    programs; Training programs)
Volunteer programs:
  contract in, 116
  full-time coordinator for, 11
  recruitment for, 11–12, 67, 100
Voter turnout, 49t, 54t
Voting blocs, 55t

Wages:
  for teachers (*see* Teachers, salaries
    of)
  for women, 57t

Weicker, Lowell, 155
Women:
  homemakers, 71
  in labor force, 40
    home workplace, 40–41
    household adjustments, 69
    job displacement, 68
    numbers of, 66
    occupational distribution, 58t

    pay disparities, 57t
    in professions, 66–67
    self-employed, 59t, 60t
    self-esteem of, 71
    political power of, 38, 39, 56t–57t
    below poverty line, 67–68
Word processing, 103
Workweek, shortened, 29, 118
Writing curriculum, 103